# MESSAGE FROM THE AUTHOR

DEAR READER, LET me start by thanking your for purchasing this book. Because I believe that as you read and ponder the contents, you will come to the recognition that the concepts and principles presented here has the potential to change your life for the better. It will help you identify and address the myths and misconceptions you've held about yourself; and how your life views have been shaped by misleading ideas that promote life as having limitations as to what you can achieve.

We are all faced with a global pandemic that will change the world and how we engage with one another individually and universally. So, the first concept that I want to introduce you to is the concept of rebirth. What I mean by rebirth is that with every adversity comes opportunity. As we are experiencing this pandemic, some people will view this experience as having no redeeming value. But you do not have to be one of those people. Because you can use this time to reevaluate your personal values and goals and see where they might need adjusting. Living in such a busy world oftentimes causes people to lose focus on what's really important. It also causes people to become irritable, easily frustrated, and most often bored and depressed when they don't know what to do with their lives. So, I invite you to use this time to truly learn and practice the principle introduced in these pages. You don't even have to leave the comforts of your home to begin to put these principles to work for you.

Your thoughts take you every place where you go. And when you are able to control your thoughts, then you can go anyplace you want to. As opposed to going places that you don't want to go. And that's because you haven't taken control of your thoughts. Is it natural for our mind to wander? Of course, it is. However, when our mind is allowed to function that way always, then we become like a boat on the sea without a rudder to guide it to a chosen destination. When this pandemic is over, as we all hope will be soon, what will be your chosen destination? Do you want to go back to doing "business as usual"? Or do you want to explore other options that an open-mind revealed to you during these days of being shut-in. The choice is yours, and I suggest that you follow your dream and make a difference in your life and in the world.

Note: Because of this present pandemic I am not taking any speaking engagements, holding any book signings, or having any seminars. However, I am developing a website where you can schedule a consultation with me by phone. In the meantime, if you have a question you can email me at drjmck29@gmail.com and I will get back to you at my earliest convenience. I will also send you the website address upon completion.

# Is There Something You Want?

## *Take It From Me!*

# Dr. John McKinney

outskirts
press

# DEDICATION

This book is dedicated to the loving memory of my father

**John Lewis McKinney, Sr.**

My Grandparents

**Frank and Sarah Trotter**

**Anthem and Lola McKinney**

**Amanda Pearl Greening**

My Aunts

**Margo and Maxine McKinney**

My Uncle and Aunt

**William and Juanita Post**

My Godmother

**Elzee Merida**

My God-Brother

**Elder Billy Joe Forrest**

And My Dear friends

**Carolyn Jackson-Dickens**
**Anthony (Meathead) Fuller**
**Randolph (Speedy) Spears**
**Gary Brown**
**Dr. Douglas Cooper**

# TABLE OF CONTENTS

# ACKNOWLEDGEMENTS

I HAVE HAD the privilege of studying many of the world's greatest thinkers, philosophers, poets, and authors whom I owe a debt of gratitude for the knowledge and wisdom I've gained from them. Their voices are heard throughout the pages of this work, some by direct quotes, others from their messages that inspired me.

I have also had the opportunity to work with many patients throughout the years who brought me the challenges they were facing in their lives. But most of all, they brought me their trust which enabled me to learn about the many facets of human behavior, while strengthen my resolve and belief that people do have the ability to make radical changes in their lives. Their voices too resound throughout the pages of this book.

On a more personal note, I acknowledge the woman who was by my side for over four decades, and who helped me see myself in ways that I would not have imagined without her, my former partner Angela McKinney. Also, to the woman who stuck by me and stuck up for me during my formative years, my BIG sister, Sharon McKinney-Balinton. To my parents who have been and still are a source of encouragement to me, George Thompson and Cubie McKinney-Thompson. To my former professors at the Berkeley Campus of the School of Professional Psychology, especially Dr. Valeta Jenkins-Monroe who I served as a research assistant under her guidance. To my former professors at Pacific Union College, especially Dr. Timothy (Timotheus) Berry who was not only my teacher and mentor but one of my closest friends and colleagues. To my good friend and former neighbor

Dr. Douglas Mosher, who always provided me with food for thought.

To the man who inspires me each week with his thought-provoking heartfelt messages, my pastor, Dr. Edward Viljoen. I also want to thank my colleagues at Pacific Union College's Career and Counseling Center under the direction of Mr. Michael Jefferson, for all they do in helping the students and collaborating with me when I need them. To the therapists I've worked with at the Napa Valley Counseling Center. To the staff at St. Helena Hospital. To the staff, volunteers, and officers of my law enforcement community for the camaraderie we share at the Napa Highway Patrol office, under the dynamic leadership of our commander, Captain John Blencowe. Also, to my riding-along partners, Roger Umbdenstock, Peter Reizman, Leslie Burma, Elizabeth Hewlett, and Officer Trinity Parr.

To those who call me dad, to those who call me brother, to those who call me their favorite uncle, and to all the members of my wonderful extended family who are the descendants of those seven spectacular Sandifer sisters, Waddie Mama, Mama Josie, Sweet Blake, Mama Em, Mama Sally, Aunt Nauv, and Aunt Tiensy. To the Greening family descendants. To my aunt and uncle, Evelyn and Charles Davis, and to my aunt Maurine McKinney-Stubblefield, and their families. To my childhood neighbor and best friend, Elumbe (Juman) Wagner, who was like a big brother to me. To my close neighbors Pat, Shannon and Steve, Brenda, Dan and Gina, I love our time together on the porch.

Last but not least, to my book analyst, Corrine Casanova of Daily House Media; to my publishing consultant, Jamie Belt; to my author representative, Jamie Rath; to all of the bank tellers, postal workers, grocery store clerks, carwash attendants, restaurant wait staff; to the Golden State Warriors and Oakland A's parking lot attendants, ticket sellers and checkers, and concessionaires; to the Vitners and Chardonnay Golf course personnel, and all of my golfing buddies; and to everyone who greets me with a warm smile whom I met along the way during my daily walks around town.

And to you, the reader, who is willing to make changes in your life, that I believe will help change the world for the better.

# Is There Something You Want?
# PREFACE

AS FAR BACK as I can remember, there has been one question that has plagued me my entire life. And that is, "Why do people do what they do?" And that of course is the basic question of all behavioral scientist. And in order for me to thoroughly understand the processes of human behavior, I had to first start with myself. I had to understand what motivation was and the role desire played in conjunction with it. I had to look at my environmental factors and genetic makeup to see what roles they played in why I thought and behaved the way I did. I also had to come to an understanding of my fears and how I was coping with them and/or trying to overcome them. I must admit that initially I wasn't very successful in overcoming my fears because I had accepted them as a part of who I was. It wasn't until I had matured and was properly motivated that prompted me to face my fears head-on. But I also had to understand what was it that matured me. Was it my circumstances? Was it my associations with mature people? Was it simply chronological, that with age come maturity? Or was it my fears themselves that helped me to realize that I didn't want to live in fear anymore?

Like everyone else, I had many questions about how to go about conducting my life in a way that I found satisfying. And believe me, I tried many things that I thought would give me permanent satisfaction. But, to no avail. It wasn't until I came to the realization that the only thing that was holding me back from a self-fulfilling life was ME.

And that there was NO thing outside of myself that could bring me lasting happiness. And I'm defining happiness as feeling the freedom to express myself as I perceive myself to be. Which meant that I had to take full responsibility for developing a value system that worked for me. The system took many years for me to develop, because I had to unlearn many things that I had learned that were not meeting my personal needs or helping me to recognize my potential. And I had not availed myself to books like this one that could help me to see what I was doing that was impeding my progress toward self-fulfillment, and how to stop doing them. However, I became quite zealous in my quest to become my own person. Partly because of my father, who wasn't very helpful in assisting me on how to understand how life worked. I'm reasonably sure he had good intentions in his parenting approach. But he didn't offer up very much information that helped me to develop a sense of personal worth based on a value system that supported me being able to take charge of my life to get the things that I wanted most. I'm not ascribing blame for his actions, or lack thereof, I'm merely pointing out that I was left with another option of how to develop something on my own. And perhaps that was a big part of my maturation process. And maybe you faced a similar dilemma during your formative years. Parents can only teach what they know. And they are products of the way they were parented, and in all likelihood will use some of the same methods that were used on them.

So, what I'm about to share with you is the process I used that enabled me to develop a value system that gave my life meaning and a passion for living. That's not to say that we all want to experience the same things in life, like writing a book, as I'm doing. But it is to say that we all want to look at how we might live a more abundant life. And to express ourselves in ways that feel natural to us. So that you may have an abundance of whatever it is that you want. Whether it is an abundance of cash or an abundance of love, you start the process of getting both in the same way.

# You THINK and GROW enRICHed!

If this title seems vaguely familiar to you, then you may have heard about or read Napoleon Hill's bestselling book, "Think and Grow Rich". It is based on the acquisition of financial gains through a series of thirteen steps he devised from studying the principals used by people who had risen to great financial wealth. Unlike Hill's book, my concentration will not be solely based on achieving financial wealth, although that may be your sole purpose for reading this book. My focus is on helping you enrich all aspects of your life by using the combined principles of Hill's work along with that of metaphysical concepts, psychological interpretations, as well as the use of religious and philosophical metaphors. I will give an updated version of Hill's model and include these other modalities for a deeper level of understanding of the thirteen principles. If you are not familiar with metaphysics, don't worry, you will have an understanding of the relevance of it as we proceed.

As you approach the reading of this book, I would ask that you treat it as your own personal therapy session. If you've never seen a professional therapist, then let me say that first and foremost the therapeutic encounter is conducted in a non-judgmental environment. The objective is not to berate you, but rather to help you better understand why you do the things you do, or why you don't do the things you ought to do in order to live a fulfilling life. Secondly, I would ask that you take seriously the exercises I offer to help you synthesize the concepts presented. If you're like me, there are probably some things that you need to unlearn, or not accept as useful anymore, and these exercises are designed to help you with that also. Some people do not like to do exercises, and if you're one of them then don't do them. However, understand why you do not want to do them. It more than likely goes back to a thought that you've held onto that says you do not like doing exercises. And until you are willing to change that thought, then you'll continue to not want to do them. But, who know, perhaps if you try doing them, you might discover that you not only enjoy them, but that you are able to use your findings about your "self" to your advantage. Thirdly, I would ask that you not overthink these new ideas by placing them into your current system of reason and logic in hopes that you can accept them. Instead of overthinking these concepts, try to imagine them as if they were something that are useful. In this way you will begin to extract the significance aspects from them that are applicable to you. If some idea or concept resonates with you, take it as a sign that there is something there that is potentially useful for you to benefit from. Remember it is this current system that you have that holds you captive to where you are. So, in order to revamp it you will need to THINK outside the box. And this doesn't mean that everything you find reasonable and logical currently to be unreasonable and illogical; it simply means that sometimes when new ideas run counter to your prevailing thoughts it might make it easier for you to dismiss it rather than explore the possibility. Life is not stagnant, and neither should your thoughts and ideas remain stagnant about the evolutionary process in your own life.

# INTRODUCTION

I HAVE ALWAYS enjoyed picking up a new book and opening its cover to see what the author has to present that I can think about and talk about to someone later. I seem to always anticipate that there will be something specifically there written for me that will not just add to my knowledge base, but that will change me as a person for the better. I remember hearing a story of a multi-millionaire attending a seminar on obtaining wealth. There was a young man who recognized him and went up to him and asked, "Sir, with all of your knowledge of obtaining wealth, why are you attending this seminar?". The millionaire responded, "Son, if I can learn just one new thing here that I can practice, then I will have considered my attendance at this seminar most beneficial to me". That's the approach I take when picking up a new book, and it is in hopes that it is the approach you take while reading this one. The principles presented here are not new, nor are they hard to understand, nor are they difficult to practice. In fact, you already know them at your subconscious level, even though you may not consciously acknowledge them for what they are. And you also practice them, even though you may not practice them with consciousness, and therefore are not taking full advantage of their benefits. And this is where _understanding_ comes in. There is a biblical verse found in Proverbs 4:7 that states, "with all your getting, get understanding." How true, because it is understanding that makes the difference between wealth and impoverishment, between joy and despair, between self-awareness and self-delusion. This book is designed to help you gain the *understanding* you need to use these life principles in a self-fulfilling way. All you need is an open-mind and a willing spirit to get actively involved in determining what it is that you want and realizing that what you want is actually a part of your unique self-expression and therefore very attainable.

## A Rose by any other Name Would Smell Just as Sweet

The premise of this book is to help you tap into your higher consciousness, or subconscious mind. It is believed by many behavioral scientists, philosophers, metaphysicians, and religionist that the subconscious mind is the portal to the realm of Divine Intelligence. Put another way, it is the part of man that knows itself to be the creator of the realities it experiences. It is the source that supplies all of the ingredients that man uses to experience the world as he does. It is given many names, some personal and some abstract, but the reference is essentially the same. Physical scientist may refer to it as energy or universal power, behavioral scientist may use terms such as the inner-being or superconscious; philosophers may refer to it as Divine Consciousness or Eternal Spirit; metaphysicians may refer to it as Divine Spirit, Infinite Intelligence or Life Force; and religionist may refer to it as God, Allah, or Jehovah. But whatever the name that one uses, it refers to a power that not only created everything that exists in the physical realm, but also sustains and controls it. And it is further stipulated by the New Thought Movement that man is an expression of this Creator, and therefore possesses the same divine nature, which is in essence his true nature. The name you ascribe to something characterizes it and gives it a particular significance. The reason why this concept of associating a name with certain characteristics is important is because it helps define the nature of the relationship. A woman who calls her husband "sweetheart" or "darling" regularly is more likely to have a closer endearing relationship to her husband than a woman who refers to her husband as "dumb ass" regularly. Now there are exceptions to these names people use when referring to people they are in relationships with. They could be culturally based, which means they carry a different meaning from one culture to another. Or, they could be situationally based, meaning that the name is associated with a situation that both parties were involved in, and from it a pet name was derived. So, the woman who refers to her husband as "dumb ass" may only use it in private with her husband as a sort of humorous gesture. Whereas, the woman who refers to her husband by that name in public as a means of being scornful, probably holds some deep resentments toward her husband. So, by ascribing a name to your "Higher Power", means you will more than likely have certain attributes associated with it that you can personally identify with. And it can also serve as a means of creating an emotional bond between you and the Spiritual Essence that is invisible to your senses.

It's not a bad idea at this time to examine your concept of a Supreme Power, which for simplification purposes I'll refer to as God, without any preconceived ideas attached to the name. Look at **Appendix A** in the back of the book and answer the questions as best you can and see what your perspective of God is or is not. The idea is to help you identify what the sources were that helped shape your thoughts around the concept of God. Even if you don't acknowledge the existence of a God, it is no harm in examining where this notion came from. Either way, your attitude and approach to life are determined by the conclusions you've reached about the concept of a Higher Power. And if you go on the premise that God acknowledges you as a unique individual, then it should not be incomprehensible to think that your concept of God would be unique to you.

## Got any Spare Change?

If, as the old adage goes, the only thing constant in life is change, then changing your behavior may not necessarily require as much effort as you might think since everything around you is changing already. The governing aspect of life is that it operates according to a cycle that keeps things moving in a forward direction at all times. And one of the main reasons some people are so resistant to change is because it moves them away from their current established comfort zone. Which means to them that as soon as they think they've gotten themselves together, it's time to move to higher ground. Yes, it does require some effort to get the ball rolling, but once you get it started, you'll be pleasantly surprised at how things will seem to fall into place. You have already exerted some effort in purchasing this book and opening the cover. Which probably wasn't all that hard. The next step in exerting effort will be to suspend some of your current beliefs about how you currently think things work. Because if you've always wanted something and don't have it, it's because you don't understand how to get it. Or you think you know how to get it, but there is something impeding your progress, which in all likelihood is your established comfort zone. That may sound simplistic, but it's based on the belief system that you are currently using to obtain the things you want. In other words, your reality is based on your perceptions, or level of awareness. The only things that exist in your reality are the things you are aware of. This doesn't mean that everything you are aware of you care about. In fact, it's probably just the opposite. Because there are so many things that the average person is aware of, it would be overwhelming to care a great deal about most of it. However, that is the purpose of why we are having these sessions, to help you prioritize what you do care about among all the things you are aware of so that you can use those things to take control of what shows up in your reality.

Living in a world of high technology, widespread information, and a vast amount of entertainment options, it's no wonder many people have become distracted in knowing or even examining what their priorities are. Some people are so hooked on gossip that they can't seem to go one day without getting on social media. Many young people are so hooked on technology that it's not unusual to see a group of them sitting in a pizza parlor not talking to each other but glued to their cellphones. Texting has gotten so prominent that laws have been passed in an attempt to keep people from doing it while driving. And don't let me get started on the entertainment business. Have you noticed how enormous entertainment has become? Entertainers are some of the highest paid people in the world. Perhaps that's what holds the fascination with these people who entertain them. Because not only do people want to be entertained, they also want to know about the entertainers' personal lives. I imagine it's normal for people to be curious and inquisitive about the background of the people they admire. But, to become consumed on the sordid details of these people's everyday lives seem preposterous to me. And it doesn't seem to matter if the gossip about the entertainer is good or bad, people just want to have something to talk about. I remember when I worked for a municipality in the San Francisco Bay Area many years ago. I overheard two of my co-workers talking very emotionally about someone who had died. Their story was touching, and I even felt sorry for the husband who had lost his beloved wife. Little did I know until later that day they were talking about a character in a soap opera. I thought to myself, they probably didn't shed a tear when their neighbor died, if they even knew their neighbor's name than they did over a fictitious character. I'm not suggesting that you not let shows touch your emotional buttons, I'm only pointing out that you may be carrying things a bit too far when you begin to regard these fictional characters as people that you think you know. There are numerous mind-numbing reality shows that keep people's minds preoccupied with worthless information. It's not that you have to cut yourself off from things you enjoy, but you would do well to ask yourself, why do you enjoy what you enjoy. If you are deriving enjoyment out of something because you're bored, then you would do well to try and understand why you feel bored. The answer that you may come up with is that you are not connected with any real purpose in your own life. And without that sense of purpose you may have lost your passion and boredom now sits in its place. So, you try to manufacture some passion by indulging in entertainment to the point of making it a top priority. And the producers of these so-called reality shows love you for it.

# Let Me Entertain You

I once had a patient come into my office claiming he was suffering from depression. And my diagnosis confirmed that he was. But it was conveniently self-induced. I soon discovered that the primary source of his depression was caused by "his" team losing the super bowl, which happens to be a football game. He claimed that it was his team even though he was not the coach, or even an assistant coach; nor was he the general manager, not an owner or shareholder; he was not even the water boy. In fact, he didn't work for the organization at all. But he thought that by being a loyal fan entitled him to claim the team as his own. And their loss was probably more devastating to him than it was to the players themselves. At least the players got paid for being there even if they didn't win the game. Don't get me wrong, I'm all for entertainment. I enjoy going to a sporting event. Even though the pandemic coronavirus has suspended play in sports indefinitely. But, rest assured, I'm not going to lose any sleep if either of those two teams don't win a game. Because it's just a game! But when you take entertainment to a level that involves the way it makes you feel about yourself, then you've taken it much too far. And the entertainment industry relies on this in order for you to keep them in BIG business. That's why there is so much media hype before, during, and after a game than the actual time it takes to play the game. I find it rather amusing that commentators will come on after the game I just watched to tell me what I just saw. I guess if I was not entertained enough by the game, I guess I could be entertained by these game analysts. But whatever they have to say does nothing to change the outcome of the game. Go figure. But, seriously, this method is a ploy by the networks to take entertainment beyond the notion of just being entertained to making it appear to have a sense of personal relevance. It's the same method employed by the creators of reality shows; to give people the illusion that they are personally knowledgeable about the lives of people they don't know. The thing about most reality shows is that they take people out of their own reality into a world of insignificance. Imagine if people knew as much about the people in their own neighborhood as they claim to know about the characters on TV. How do you think that would affect their thinking about what's important? Or is that asking too much of people to actually get out and get to know their neighbors? We all get distracted from time to time, and distractions are okay in your spare time. But heavy doses of entertainment that people are exposed to regularly keep their minds preoccupied with "stuff" that's not very relevant to getting them active in their own lives. Which in turn fosters the philosophy of the society that wants to keep the masses in conformity, that way they remain fairly predictable. We'll look at this topic of conformity and how it affects your life in a subsequent session.

## Don't Give Up, Give In!

When you give up on something, you are basically convincing yourself that the universe, or some forces outside of yourself have conspired to keep you for doing what you want and obtaining what you desire. That idea is a myth. If anything, the universe and all the forces that control it acts in your favor in every way. Think about it! What if the sun were to come 20 or 30 thousand miles closer to the earth or 20 to 30 thousand miles further away? We would experience unbearable temperatures that would make it impossible for us to survive as a species. Or what if gravity suddenly suspended its activity. There would be nothing to keep anything in place. These are just a couple of examples of how the forces that control the universe helps each and every one of us. So, don't give up on the idea that you can do or have what you want because there is nothing that is keeping it from you, but you. But you will need to give in to the idea that the forces that control the universe do so according to an Infinite Intelligence. This Intelligence knows everything there is to know about how to align your thoughts with the understanding it needs to accomplish whatever it is that you desire. By giving in to this concept of an Infinite Intelligence, you acknowledge that there is a means that goes beyond human reasoning alone that will enable you to reach your highest potential. Because if you knew how to reach your highest potential according to your reasoning, you would have done so already. While this book does appeal to your human reasoning, it does not rely totally on it as a means of getting you to grasp the enormity of what's possible for you. This has to come from a place deep inside your psyche that knows it is directly connected to Infinite Intelligence.

So, our sessions will be about changing your perceptions so that they will include the things that you want most out of life. Getting what you want out of life by mastering your thoughts and practicing new behaviors is not for the faint of heart. It requires patience, consistency and persistence. The faint of heart settles for as little as possible without high expectations for themselves. The faint of heart lay around waiting for something better to happen, knowing full well that nothing will. Now, you may think this requires a lot of effort. But it takes no more effort to learn to master your thoughts to get what you want than it does to complain about not having what you want. Many people who don't get what they want will oftentimes go to great lengths to let others know about it. If you are a driver, think about when you were first learning how to drive. It probably didn't seem like much of an effort after you got your driver's permit. Probably because you were highly motivated; and as you began to experience the benefits of being mobile you felt that the effort you put into learning how to drive was worth it. Well, this book will help give you mobility of thought as it pertains to developing your mental prowess, and you will begin to experience the benefits even before you have completely manifested your desires.

## It's Called the Unconscious Because It is Unconscious!

I will briefly mention the work of psychologist Dr. Carl Jung as it pertains to individual thoughts versus thoughts that are a part of a collective. Individual thoughts are the ones that you might say comes off the top of your head. They are thoughts that may come from long held dreams, or thoughts that reflect something in your personality that seeks expression, like going skydiving. Jung postulates that there is also something he calls the collective unconsciousness. This is a consciousness that you hold unconsciously because it has been established and accepted by people you are in agreement with. It doesn't have to be factual, only presented and adhered to by the dominate society, culture, religious organization, governmental agency, etc. An example of this phenomenon was when the majority of earthlings held the belief that the world was flat. This was the prevailing theory, and people consciously accepted it and it became embedded in the subconscious minds of those who were alive at that time. It wasn't until this theory was disproved that the collective unconsciousness regarding a flat earth was dismantled. So, what does this mean to you? It means that you too have been subjected to things that were present in your environment that you may have accepted as truth, that really were not. Remember when I mentioned conformity earlier and how it is used by societies as a means to reasonably predict what people might do in a given situation? Well, the collective consciousness is part of a system to get people to conform to an idea or concept that holds a group together. Whether it's political, or religious, or social in nature, the objective is the same. Think about what was mentioned about the news, and even social media. Their main objective is to present you with something that appears believable. And there is nothing inherently wrong with that. The problem I see is when the collective consciousness permeates a society and the prevailing thought is that you have to settle for what you get out of life and that you have little to no control over what that is. Hogwash! Don't allow other's thinking to influence you into settling for less than what you want. You do not have to be a part of the mass thinking that abundance is out of your reach. Our sessions should help you to identify some of the thoughts you acquired from the collective consciousness that do not serve your goal to reach your highest potential.

# Mental Updating

There is a passage in the Christian bible that says, "don't put new wine into old wineskins.". Meaning that it is unwise to try to make new ideas conform to an outdated belief system. No one wants to think that their belief system is outdated. But, the truth of the matter is, that if you aren't cognizant of the "signs of the times" then your system may be in need of an update. The signs of the times simply refer to the idea that everything is in flux and moving to a higher level. Remember life never goes backward, it is constantly moving forward and expanding all manner of energy and matter. Or as the saying goes, "The only thing that remains constant, is change.". And change has many ways of being demonstrated. Some changes are quite overt and easier to observe, while others are very subtle and do not draw much attention and therefore are less obvious. But, the important thing to remember is that you are a part of all the changes that are taking place around you, whether wittingly or unwittingly. So, as you approach these concepts and ideas that may sound new to you, I ask that you keep an open and curious mind and a willing spirit. Willing to pursue the depths of truth that is revealed to you as you read and digest the words into the inner sanctum of your consciousness. Therein lies your transformation.

Each session is designed to build on previous concepts presented, although they are to be taken as a whole. In other words, you may understand how to use autosuggestions or affirmations, but without understanding how to use your imagination effectively it will affect your overall effort in achieving your desires. Some sessions may be more extensive in giving a broad perspective of the principle involved. This could mean that you may want to take each subsection separately and contemplate its meaning for the purpose of clarity before moving on to another concept. You should move though this material at a pace that's comfortable for you for maximum comprehension. In other words, don't gloss over something if you don't get it on the first reading. It could be that your mind is not responsive because it is not fully focused at the moment. So, if you need to take a break to think about something else that may be on your mind, then take a moment. Remember, "Rome was not built in a day.". Which means that if something is to be done correctly, then you should give it the proper amount of time to develop. As you probably can already tell, I like using quotations; and you will find them throughout the pages of this book, usually with a meaning I ascribe to it. Such as the quote, "You can't see the forest for the trees". In psychological terms this would mean that you cannot see the options in your life and the opportunities they offer you to reach your maximum potential because you are captive to your present-day circumstances and the ritualistic behaviors you are used to performing. Sound familiar?

So, to get started with our first session I will ask you to consider the question that is constantly before you, what do YOU really want? I say that this question is constantly before you because in every situation you find yourself in you have to address this question on some level of your thinking. On the surface it may seem like a question that can be answered with a relatively simple response. And you may have a simple answer, like "I want to be happy". However, is this a conditioned response, or one that has a meaningful definition that sees happiness as a state of mind rather than a situation where all of the external conditions appear favorable to you. Upon further investigation you will discover that there are many layers to this question, and this is where we'll begin our quest for the answers, by peeling back the layers. But before starting our journey together I will remind you that you will need two things. The first is an open mind, to collect the gems of wisdom you discover. And the second thing you'll need is a curiosity that will allow you to conceive of the many possibilities for personal growth. If curiosity killed the cat, then let's make the cat your old antiquated version of yourself that you will replace with a new and improved version.

## What Time Is It?

The time is NOW! This statement is not a simple cliché in an attempt to alarm you into some sense of urgency to act desperately. It is mentioned to draw your attention to the fact that, like many others, you may be trapped in the concept of time as being divisible. However, there is only one time, and that time is always now. To even think about something that you believe has passed, you have to think about it in the present. The same applies to the future. And even though time is a constant without division, like gravity, it can serve as a useful tool when executed properly. The primary reason people procrastinate is because they are under the impression that there will be a better time other than now to get something done. Because if they thought that the present moment was the best time to do it then they probably would. But what better time is there to take control of the only thing you have the capability of having complete control over, your own self. There is no reason for you to wait on getting the most out of life when life is offering it to you right NOW! Life knows no time or space. These are man-made constructs used for the purpose of reference points. So, it goes that, you are either here or over there. Or, you have a past and a future. These are references to space and time. But Life is everywhere all the time. So, these concepts have no bearing on Life's ability to make things happen in the present moment, because the present moment is the only time there is, and right here is the only place there is. If you think of the concept of space as having two separate conditions, here and there, then in order to get from here to there means that they have to be connected, or it would be impossible for you to get there. The same with time. In order to get to tomorrow, you will have to be in the present. The old saying, "Don't put off tomorrow what you can do today!" is apropos for the approach you must take in order to change the course of your life in the direction that brings you the fulfillment you so richly deserve. Because whatever you do today effects what happens in this thing called tomorrow, because of the interconnection. Another saying that goes, "Time is of the Essence" can also be applicable when you begin to use time as your most valued treasure and seek to use it responsibly. And responsibly means setting your priorities so that insignificant things do not take precedence over significant ones. Because using the concept of time as a tool means that it can be used either constructively or destructively. The last quote I'll use here about time is, "Don't let time pass you by". I would modify this quotation by saying, "Don't let opportunity pass you by." The implication is the same in both quotations in that if you are not using your time responsibly then you are missing out on the opportunities that avail themselves to you. Oh, there is one more, "Time waits for no man". In this quotation, time implies that change is constantly occurring all around you. Therefore, you must remain in an adaptability mode as things change, or you will get left behind using an outdated ineffective mode of handling these new situations.

Even though time is a mental construct and a valuable tool that can be used to better your life conditions, don't treat it irreverently as it pertains to you getting what you want. Time is part of a developmental process that brings about the manifestations of your desires as you do your part in maintaining your focus and persistence in doing whatever is necessary to follow the process to completion. You may feel like you are not making headway, or even losing ground in some areas of your life when you commit yourself to something you strongly desire. It may seem like things are not happening fast enough. But don't despair, because your commitment represents your union with Infinite Intelligence. And the more you feel the presence of this Intelligence working in your life, the less you will care about anything that stand as a potential obstacle. If you look at history, you will find that there have been those who have lost fortunes and even given-up their fortunes in order to obtain something greater. The story of Moses in the bible is an example of a man who could have reigned in the courts of Egypt and enjoyed the fruits of the good life. But rather chose to see life on a bigger scale and became an advocate and deliverer for the less fortunate.

# THOUGHTS - THE POWER OF CHOICE

HAVE YOU EVER stopped and asked yourself, "Where do thoughts come from?"? Are they a product of our sensory intake? Certainly, we have experiences and have thoughts about them. In fact, you can't have an experience without having a thought about it. But, does the thought precede the experience, or vice-versa? Neuroscientist attributes thoughts as part of an energy system stemming from the central nervous system and the peripheral nervous system. Which has two parts, the somatic and autonomic nervous systems. These two systems control such things as your heart, lungs, digestive system, muscles, and so on. And they do so without the aid of you having to consciously think about it. Whereas, the central nervous system is said to receive all incoming data from the sense organs and causes a reaction depending on the relevance of the information. It is believed that the central nervous system uses a data bank to help determine what response might be most appropriate for the situation. So, the question becomes, how did the data bank get established, if this data bank truly represents all of our thoughts? The new thought concept ascribes our thoughts as being lodged in the subconscious mind. Which I take to mean the part of our mind that detects energy flow and systemic patterns in our environment and formulates them into conscious thoughts. Perhaps neuroscientist and the new thought pundits are saying the same thing but using different terminology. Which leads me to the next question, "can our conscious thoughts override our somatic and autonomic nervous system?" Behavioral scientist uses a form of psychological monitoring called biofeedback as a therapeutic method to help individuals become aware of how their body is functioning. The purpose is designed to assist the individual in controlling certain aspects of their body with energy producing thoughts. And people have been known to lower their blood pressure and change their brain waves using biofeedback methods. This is a clear indication that the thought precedes the event once the person is made aware of what they need to think about in order to change what is happening.

## Chickens or eggs?

All of this may sound like the argument of which came first, the chicken or the egg. But this concept is at the heart of igniting every change that has or ever will take place. It is established on the concept that we do not live in a physical world. We live in a physically produced world. Produced by what? An Infinite Intelligence that consists of everything that is needed to create and sustain that which It creates. Which means that everything has been perfectly thought out, from the greatest sun to the smallest atom, in order for the physical world to exist indefinitely. And the same thing applies to you and me. We are a part of creation that can think things into existence in conjunction with this Infinite Intelligence. New Thought postulates that human beings are expressions of this Infinite Intelligence and therefore are capable of creating their own experiences according to the choices they make. This means we have a thought about our experiences before we actually create them. Which is the only way we are able to define what the experience is. Remember, nothing exists for you that you are not aware of. So, at some level in your mind, you think about having an experience, and it comes to pass. To think that your experiences come first would mean that you think you are a victim of your circumstances. That the world produces random events that you just happen to get caught in the crosshairs. You may even try to explain the reverse order of events happening prior to thoughts by means of comparison. That is, what if someone else had a similar experience and you took your definition of your experience from theirs? Such as a person inheriting a million dollars and you are bequeathed a million dollars from your rich uncle. The fact still remains that you would not be aware that there is a similarity between the two events if you hadn't had the experience in thought first.

## You make me sick!

You may have heard the term psychosomatic disorder. It is a mental malady that produces physical symptoms when a person *believes* they have an illness. In other words, it refers to people who think themselves sick. Conversely, there are occasions when people are prayed for and become cured of a physical illness without medical assistance. The amazing work of renown author and physician Dr. Gerald Jampolsky with cancer patients attests to this phenomenon. The idea that thoughts are a part of an energy source that sets into motion the process of physical manifestation in spite of current conditions is encouraging to those who have lost hope in believing things will never change for them. This concept is fundamental for therapist in my profession who practice cognitive behavioral therapy (CBT) and see it as the most influential component in changing behavior. Some CBT practitioners use what I call the Holy Trinity model for behavioral changes. Thought + Desire + Imagination = Manifestation, (Self-expression). The fundamental process is:

The more frequent you visit a thought about something the greater it increases your desire to revisit that thought.

The more intense your desire becomes in entertaining that thought, the more it ignites the imagination to preserve the probability of the thought actually occurring.

The more clarity the imagination gives to the perceived desire for the thought to occur will produce a heightened feeling for its fulfillment.

And when the feeling can no longer be contained within the confines of the imagination, the feeling is united with the imagination's construct of putting the desire into motion using all the energy of the mind that it needs to manifest the desire.

This of course is a summary version of the theory. But, as you will see later on, it is a workable model that we will expand upon as we delve into the "how to" which will bring this concept into sharper focus. But for now, try to imagine this concept of thoughts preceding experiences and see if you can get a sense of the beneficial value of why this process works. The world that we live in is a self-perpetuating body. That means that the principles used for the purpose of governing and sustaining itself must be the same on the micro level as it is on the macro level.

## The Choice is Yours

When you conceive of thoughts as energy, it helps you to better understand that thoughts are not always passive, or even innocuous. They hold the power that affect your choices. People base their choices on a perception that is believed to hold some beneficial value. In other words, we all make our choices based on them being self-serving. However, this does not mean that all choices are selfish in nature. The person who works as a nurse, or a police officer, or any profession where others are benefitted from the performance of their duties may do so for a paycheck; but there are those who do so because it makes them *feel* good about themselves in helping others. Both are self-serving, one is for money and the other is for a feeling. Some entertainers like the comedienne, George Wallace, would do what they do even if they weren't paid handsomely for it. George commented that from the time he was a youngster he loved to make people laugh. Which brings us to a couple of other questions. Are all choices based on feelings? and do people make choices that make them feel bad? To the first question I would venture to say that all choices are based on an anticipated feeling based on the association it has with personal values. In other words, a person who believes that doing something that coincides with their beliefs will more than likely make a choice in favor of supporting their values. And they do so in anticipation of their choice producing a good feeling based on having done something they believe is right. Even a somewhat neutral feeling is considered an okay feeling to have even though it may only minutely arouse ones' emotions. Conversely, if one makes a choice contrary to their value system, then they will anticipate feeling "bad" or guilty because their belief is that they are in violation of their value system. The answer to the second question, do people make choices that make them feel bad was partially answered in the last response, yes, they do, even if it puts them at odds with what they claim to believe. But I will add that people will also make choices based on what is call a secondary benefit. An example is when a person chooses to remain ill because of the poor lifestyle choices they continue to make, but they seek to gain sympathy from the people they tell about their pain. The secondary benefit being the sympathy they garner from others and interpreting that sympathy as caring. So, their choice is made to gain sympathy at the expense of making healthy lifestyle choices.

## Courage under fire

Sometimes in life, we are required to take a stand and make what may be perceived by others as a very difficult choice. This type of choice is generally broad in scope and made in order to make a statement. This type of choices is heavily influenced by the purpose we see for our life. And the clearer we are about what purpose we serve in our human existence makes our life choices most profound. I'm reminded of a story I heard about an elderly Jewish man in a Nazi prison camp. When all the men were lined up one morning, the prison guards were selecting every other man to be sent to the gas chambers. As they came down the line the old man saw what was going on and knew he would be spared while the young man standing next to him would be executed. The old man quietly slipped behind the young man and switched places with him so that the young man's life would be spared. Ordinarily one might think that someone would cling to their own life instead of sparing the life of another. However, when you see your purpose in that moment, it causes you to make a choice that supports your purpose. Even if it's at the expense of your own life. It is these situations that demonstrates how well you have convinced yourself that your beliefs are truly worth living and dying for. It is the link between accepting your purpose in life and the will to follow it to the letter that give one the courage to make a difficult choice under fire. However, when we are not sure what our purpose is, or have not established life goals for ourselves, then our life choices may be tenuous at best and subject to our perception of what we might perceive as socially accepted behaviors.

## The Storehouse

All thoughts are housed in the Storehouse of Infinite Possibilities. This storehouse is always open for business and supplies its visitors with whatever they request. It even has a return policy, that if you take away a possibility that's not to your liking, you can always return it at any time for a full refund with no questions asked. The only catch is, there are no duplicate items. Each thought is unique and comes with complete instructions on how to best utilize it. Sometimes customers don't follow these instructions and wonder why their product isn't working properly. Like the story of the man who thought that God was going to save him from the flood that occurred in his hometown. He had climbed upon the roof of his house and waited for his deliverance. When a man in a rowboat came by, he excused the man and told him God was going to save him. Then another man in a motorboat came by, and he excused that man also. Finally, a helicopter flew over and lowered the ladder for him to climb up to safety. But the man refused. Then the inevitable happened, the water rose, and the man drowned. When he got to heaven, he asked God, "I thought that when I accepted you as my Savior that you would save me." God replied to the man, "Who do you think sent the rowboat, the motorboat, and the helicopter?". Following the instructions quite often means giving up your preconceived ideas about how you think things are *supposed* to work.

## The Law of Cause and Effect

The choices that you make are associated with certain outcomes, this process is commonly known as cause and effect. If you chose to jump off of a twenty-story building onto a concrete street, it wouldn't matter what your thoughts about gravity are as they pertain to giving you a free pass to avoid injury or death by suspending its function of bringing you down. Because any reasons that you can come up with to get that free pass will run contrary to the laws of physics. The only exception would be your <u>absolute</u> conviction that this act coincides with your life purpose. And I say absolute because there can be no shred of doubt at all. The law of cause and effect is established in both the physical domain as well as the invisible domain. The invisible domain being that which operates behind the scenes of all physical manifestation. Like the electrical currents that run through a conduit from a generator to a light bulb. The light coming from the bulb is the *effect* that is *caused* by making contact with the electricity. Simply stated, the law of cause and effect means that everything that effects your life, has a direct cause. And every cause that you create will have a predictable result, even if you have no clue as to what that result may be. In religious circles it may be referred to as Karma; or the Golden Rule. In informal circles it may be stated as, "what goes around, comes around". But, the generality of the law means that if you want something specific to experience in your life, then you must administer the appropriate cause for the effect to take place. The more you recognize the value of this law, the more impervious you will be toward so-called unexpected events. Because no event is without cause.

## Think Back When

I would like for you to go back in time and try to remember any long-held thoughts you had about the people you grew up around. What were they like? What do you recall about their personalities and/or character? What habitual behaviors did you notice them performing? What did they seem to be most interested in? What do you recall as one of the happiest experiences you had growing up that involved another person? What about the saddest experience? What do you recall wanting to be when you grew up? If you ever played "make believe", what or who were you? If you were to describe yourself as a child, what descriptive words would you use? What were the biggest challenges you faced as a child? When you got upset, what do you recall doing to soothe your emotions? What do you recall about your behavior when you were in the presence of others who were much older? Younger? In a position of authority? Who had physical characteristics that were different from yours and what did you think about those differences?

After you have answered these questions from your childhood, go back over them and compare them with your present-day experiences of being around others and how you relate to them. How are your perceptions of people different as an adult? How are they the same?

# DESIRE – THE GREAT MOTIVATOR

WHAT YOU REALLY want is determined by your desires. You may not always be sure why you want what you want, but you can always be sure that you will not accomplish or acquire anything unless you have a desire for it. Desires start initially as a thought about something and then the thought moves to a feeling that you get from wanting something for whatever reason you think you might want it. And then it becomes a *burning* desire when it is elevated to the emotional level where you cannot see yourself without it. In other words, failure to obtain your desire is not an option. It can be described as a healthy obsession if the desire matches the need for self-expression according to your true nature. It becomes an unhealthy obsession when it stands in violation of your true nature and caters to your ego. The difference being that your true nature is an expression that comes from your soul, or spirit. Your ego is your mental construct of what you think you ought to be based on the opinions, suggestions, and criticisms of others. From a financial perspective, Napoleon Hill states that there are six ways to turn desire into gold.

1. Be specific, know exactly how much money it is that you want.
2. Know what it is that you are willing to give in return for the money. What is your investment?

3. Set a time limit.
4. Create a definitive plan and put it into action whether you feel like you are ready or not. (Brainstorm, meditate, or do whatever you need to do to come up with a plan that you can begin to act on immediately.)
5. Put everything on paper, amount of money, timeframe, your investment, and your plan of action.
6. Read your written statement aloud when you arise in the morning and at night just before bedtime. As you read your statement feel yourself already in possession of the money you desire.

A poem by Jessie B. Rittenhouse is herein quoted because it captures the relationship between you and Life and how It responds to your desires for wealth.

"I bargained with Life for a penny,
And Life would pay no more,
However I begged at evening
When I counted my scanty store.

"For Life is a just employer,
He gives you what you ask,
But once you have set the wages,
Why, you must bear the task.

"I worked for a menial's hire,
Only to learn, dismayed,
That any wage I had asked of Life,
Life would have willingly paid."

When you bargain with Life for what you desire, you must be clear in your own mind. Think of it as though you were going shopping for a new outfit for a specific occasion, such as a wedding. If you are a smart shopper, you would know what sizes you needed, you would look in the formal wear department, and you would know how much you were willing to spend. There is very little difference when shopping for wealth. Because as you become mentally clear, your desires move from wishful thinking to taking the shape for their manifestation. Belief, plus a burning desire puts things in motion toward fulfillment. And, your beliefs must include the feeling that you deserve to have your financial goals met. And you do!

But you probably desire more things than just being wealthy. And if you are like most people, you want to be wealthy because you want to use money to enhance your relationships. Why have lots of money if you don't have people around that you care about to enjoy it with? It's like having a big banquet and no one is sitting at the table but you. Money, like most things, is a tool to be used for the purpose of expressing who you are in relationship to it. The same can be said about money as can be said about a partner. And that is, the person you are in partnership with says as much about you as it does the person that you are with. Which means that what you attract to yourself are the qualities that reflect something about you. So, how you utilize money is also a reflection of something in your character that you are expressing.

## Who Wants to Be a Millionaire?

Some people may think that having a few million dollars will guarantee them a comfortable life. But what truly constitutes a comfortable life? Here's where that clarity thing comes in. Millionaires aren't exempt from life stressors, challenges, or misfortunes. They can and do experience the stress of deadlines; the challenges of finding meaning in what they are doing or not doing; and the misfortune of losing a loved one far sooner than expected. In fact, many millionaires experienced suffering and hardships before setting out on their path of creating wealth for themselves. Oftentimes it is our struggles that prompts us to take certain actions. Paraphrasing something I heard noted physician Dr. Bernie Siegel once say, is that the pain and suffering you experience can be your labor pains in birthing a new life for yourself. In other words, don't let pain and suffering debilitate you, but rather use them to feed your inner determination to overcome them. Remember, it's not what life throws your way, but how you respond to it. If you define a comfortable life as a life that provides you with more opportunities to practice developing your personage to serve as a catalyst for good to occur in the world, then by all means make yourself comfortable. And you can do it with or without a million dollars but having a million dollars shouldn't hurt your cause. A third of the United States population is said to be living below the poverty level. Does this mean that increased incomes would solve the conditions of poverty? Not if the cause of impoverishment is not examined and addressed first. Like the old saying goes, "You can take Jethro out of the country, but you can't take the country out of Jethro." There was an old TV program that depicted what I'm describing, call the Beverly Hillbillies. The hillbillies became millionaires overnight when oil was discovered on their property. But their attitudes and perceptions on living in the big city didn't change, they just had more so-called modern stuff in addition to the stuff they brought with them from the country. And it's not just the attitudes of the people who are impoverished that needs to change, but also those who live around them and continue to allow impoverished condition to exist.

Every major city in the United States has a homeless population. And a number of people are up in arms about it. But, when it comes to building a homeless shelter, most of these people don't want one built in or near their neighborhoods. Homelessness could not be tolerated if the American people considered it appalling enough to put an end to it. But many have become desensitized to it and have accepted it as a way of life. And others have becomes so distracted with everything from terrorism to the latest gossip about the Kardashians, that their priorities have become skewed. And because homelessness in America has been used as a political meatball, most people think the government should and can do something about it. So, it is left in the hands of the very politicians who helped create the situation through the various laws and policies that keep breaking the backs of the middle-class. Most homeless people aren't former millionaires. They were working class people who were squeezed out of the job market, or who were not able to maintain their living status because of runaway inflation. If charity truly begins at home, then Americans should be taking better care of the immediate problems within its' own borders, homelessness being a major one. I didn't mean to get on a soapbox, but this does tie into what we are addressing; which is your attitude toward money and what you believe about it in relation to your desire for it, or for anything else you desire. What I'm pointing out is that when your desires go beyond personal gratification alone, you are more prone to gain the clarity needed to attract it to you.

If you want a million dollars, then desire it fully. Don't carry around contradictory thoughts, such as "I want a million dollars, BUT...." because whatever comes after the but negates the prospect of fulfilling the desire. And be clear as to why you want what you want. Use your imagination to help you see how having a million dollars will help you better express yourself as the person you really are and the person you're choosing to become. I say this because some people want a million dollars in order to make purchases that they believe will impress other people or to use money as a means of projecting a pretentious image. You should realize that life doesn't support faulty belief systems, which is one that is inconsistent with your true nature. Life may still allow you to have the million dollars even though you have a faulty belief system about how to use it properly. But, like everything else that you use for a purpose other than what it was designed for, you will not experience the level of enjoyment, peace, and contentment with it. In fact, it may even bring you more grief from constant worry about losing it, than if you never possessed it. So often people push away the things they desire because they desire them for the "wrong" reasons. I do understand that there are truly no "wrong" reasons, because "wrong" is a subjective word;

but there are reasons that may prove harmful to your psyche and can be detrimental to your overall well-being.

## Money Matters

I recall when I was a young man in my twenties, I was living my life as I pleased and doing most things that I enjoyed. I left my job at a local municipality and got my real estate license. I started out working in a small real estate office in my hometown, but shortly thereafter I landed a position with a large real estate company in Berkeley, Mason-McDuffie Company. It was quite an experience for me being exposed to lavish homes in the Berkeley hills and surrounding areas that were at the high-end of the real estate spectrum. The exposure alone was enough to trigger a desire in me to live in the lap of luxury, and I eventually did. I went from selling homes in the $10,000 range, to selling homes in the $100,000 range, which meant larger commissions. Back then a home selling for one-hundred thousand dollars was a lot of money. Those same homes now sell in the millions. Especially the ones designed by noted architects, like John Maybeck. After making enough money in listings and sells, I then got the idea that I should use some of it to invest in real estate, since I knew something about it and having seen prices of homes on the rise I thought it to be a good investment. Within a relatively short period of time I had amassed a million dollars in assets, primarily in real estate holdings. I had houses and apartments, and joint interest in a couple of buildable lots. I even started my own company, Pioneer Investment Company, and opened an office on the top floor of a new office building in my hometown. At the time, I don't recall that I felt any different toward money, or myself as a result of acquiring these assets. But I do recall the enjoyment I found in showing properties to my clients and purchasing properties for myself.

## I Gots' My 'Ligion

Then the unthinkable occurred, I found religion. Becoming religious wasn't a bad thing, it was just that I was young and naïve, and probably took things that I read in the bible too literally. Like most people who find religion, I was looking for something more to life on a deeper level. Its not that I was looking to religion to supply me with the answers that I needed to help me feel I was doing the "right" things, it was more so to help me realize my purpose in life. It wasn't that I didn't believe in God before I found religion, but my growing discontentment with short lived pleasures made me think I needed something to quench my thirst for understanding human behavior, particularly my own. So, to make a really long story shorter, at some point I started to believe that money was the root of all evil, and I began to divest myself of my properties, some even at a loss. I was gullible, and on a mission to purify myself from the evil effects of money. There was a particular story in the bible that I related to most. It was the story of a rich young ruler, who of course, I saw myself as. In this story a wealthy young man hears Jesus' message, and decides he want to be a follower. So, Jesus instructs him to sell all of his possessions, and give the proceeds to the poor, and then come follow him. I took this to mean that Jesus was saying that rich people didn't have much of a chance to make it into the kingdom of heaven because their riches got in the way of them "serving" God. By-the-way, at the time I thought that heaven was an actual physical location with pearly gate, streets of gold, and the whole nine yards. But I only partially understood the meaning of the story, in that money does have the *potential* of getting in the way of acknowledging things that are of more importance, like relationships. But later I came to realize the psychological issue Jesus was addressing. The moral of the story is that one should not use riches as a means of determining their self-worth, nor to laud it over people as a means of exerting power. Money is almost incidental to the story, but because most people see it as a powerful and universal medium that is often used inappropriately, it gives the story greater significance.

Seeking or trying to possess anything outside yourself as a measuring device to be used for developing a character that is consistent with your true nature isn't plausible. It wasn't until I became a behavioral scientist that I began to better understand that the moral values in the biblical stories are not found in their literal interpretations, but rather what they reveal about human nature. In other words, the literal interpretive process I had previously used I found to be more guilt based rather than a revelation of how the human nature effect human behaviors. As a result, I was influenced in ways that did not serve me well. Most of which stemmed from my childhood beliefs about avoiding going to that place where evildoers are sentenced for all eternity that burns with fire and brimstone. So, the real issue for me was not purging myself of money. But rather finding my own voice in interpreting that which life reveals through sacred writings and my own experiences. This valuable life lesson helped me to understand that money is a tool that should be used to support your character, and not your habits. Which we'll talk more about later, how habits can turn into addictions.

## It's as Clear as Mud

In order to attain clarity of your desires, especially when it comes to money, you would do well to look beyond the surface. How do you look beyond the surface, you ask? Banter with yourself, letting your subconscious mind serve as the proverbial inquisitive child who continually asks why each time your conscious mind produces an answer. So, if you make a statement like, "Having a million dollars will help me to live a comfortable life.", then your subconscious asks Why? "Because living a comfortable life will afford me the opportunities to do all the things I've always wanted to do". Why? "Because I'm tired of living from day-to-day and from paycheck to paycheck without experiencing any excitement in my life." Why? "Because I suppose I was never taught or encouraged to go after the things I wanted in life." Why? "Because I figured it was expected of me to settle for what was convenient and available to me at the time." Why? "Because coming from my background, I didn't have the opportunities for advancement." Why? "Because my parents never taught me the ends and outs about what it takes to live life abundantly." Why? As you can see, the conversation can go on and on and on. But, stop it when you get to the place where you can see and feel that you are primarily responsible for your attitude toward money and the position you now hold in your life without blaming other people or your circumstances. And, don't blame yourself either, because blame disempowers, and causes you to feel like a victim. And as you already know, victims are always at the mercy of others, and if you are to live abundantly you cannot be at the mercy of anyone. You can own up to being responsible for what you've done or failed to do without accusations and blame. Even feeling remorseful doesn't have to be associated with blaming. If you're like most people who lives in a society that propagates getting ahead, then you probably have succumbed to the idea that getting ahead means having more money than the next person. So, money then becomes the yardstick upon which to measure whether or not you've gotten ahead, instead of being a supplement for the expression of what you truly believe in.

If you seem to have difficulty coming up with a line of questioning about your relationship to money, take a look at **Appendix B** in the back of the book and answer those questions. As you begin to answer these questions you will begin to see a pattern about your line of thinking about money. This is good because when you can see the pattern you can generally trace your thoughts back to their origin. And when you find the origin you can question the validity of its current value to you. Now, I'm going to reiterate something that I alluded to earlier, and that is, in order for YOU to obtain wealth, you must *expect* it to come your way. You must imagine having it and then expecting it, because if you don't expect it you are merely engaged in wishful thinking. Your expectancy must reach the level of assuming you already have that which you desire. Some people say that when you assume you make an "ass out of u and me". However, there is a law at work called the *law of assumption*. It is what brings your thinking to the level of acknowledging that your desires are already met. And this line of thinking is what give credence to your acceptance of the things you desire as already existing. So, as you answer the questions in Appendix A, keep in mind that you are seeking to identify the fallacies and myths you may still hold about money. So, that you can replace the old misconceptions about money with a new image that serve you and is part of your self-expression. Remember, money is not causal, it is an effect, therefore you must supply the cause via your thinking process about it in order to receive it.

# FAITH – THE SPIRIT LIFTER

FAITH IS THE ingredient that takes the feeling of your desires and transforms them to a vibration that the subconscious uses to communicate with Infinite Intelligence. Faith is a state of mind that can be developed voluntarily through the use of autosuggestions and affirmations. Which means that you can bring any suggestion to your subconscious mind and based on the intensity of the feeling for your desire, the subconscious will act on these suggestions as though they are already in existence. Therefore, faith is the acknowledgement of your desire having already been fulfilled, prior to its physical manifestation.

Hill states that you should have faith in yourself, and in Infinite Intelligence. He makes these remarks about faith:

"Faith is the "eternal elixir" which gives life, power, and action to the impulse of thought!
"Faith is the starting point of all accumulations of riches!
"Faith is the basis of all "miracles," and all mysteries which cannot be analyzed by the rules of science!
"Faith is the only known antidote for failure!
"Faith is the element, the "chemical" which, when mixed with prayer, gives one direct communication with Infinite Intelligence.

"Faith is the element which transforms the ordinary vibration of thought, created by the finite mind of man, into the spiritual equivalent.
"Faith is the only agency through which the cosmic force of Infinite Intelligence can be harnessed and used by man."

I alluded to the law of assumption previously and now I want to expand upon it in relationship to faith. Again, the law of assumption means that you assume the thing you have faith in already exists. This faith is substantive and therefore exists in reality. It starts at your deep-seated subconscious level. And when the conscious mind touches on the subconscious mind through faith then you come to the realization that what you desire does in fact already exists. Understand that you cannot assume that something exists if you aren't aware of it. This book or your tablet that you're reading this book from only exists because you're aware of it. Even before you bought it or entered into the room and picked it up to read, you were aware of its existence. It was only after you became aware of its existence that you were able to presume ownership. The point I'm making is that the substance of your hope of obtaining this book was based on your faith that it was possible to obtain. And once you did that, you then assumed that it was attainable for you. The process is the same, whether it's for a book, a new career, the acquisition of wealth, a new relationship, or whatever you choose. Faith is the only thing that will keep you moving forward toward your desires and past your self-imposed limitations!

Some people believe that you have to be connected to some religious persuasion in order to exercise the law of assumption associated with faith. But, like gravity, this law is applicable no matter what your religious affiliation may or may not be. In fact, it probably works more effectively for people who aren't encumbered with false concepts of what Infinite Intelligence (God) likes or dislikes. However, if you think you can use this law of assumption destructively without impunity, know that you are still subjected to another law, the law of cause and effect. Which means that whatever you put (cause to happen) into the universe, the effect of it will occur to you.

The exercising of your faith is founded on your personal value system. So, as you develop a value system that portrays you as the highest version of yourself that you can perceive, then your faith will guide you in projecting your new behaviors. In that way, you allow your imagination to work in conjunction with how you consciously perceive yourself and how you desire to express that perception. The exercising of your faith toward a higher version of yourself is what builds self-confidence. And when you don't have faith in yourself, you develop low self-esteem. And low self-esteem can be a plague that causes behaviors that stunt personal growth in a way that can cause permanent mental damage if not corrected in time.

## How Esteemed is your Self-esteem?

Much of our programmed thinking came from those who we were most in proximity to, namely our parents or caregivers. Through inheritance and from our observations of behaviors we developed a sense of human characteristics that exemplified different ways of being. If both your parents had high self-esteem it exposed you to behaviors that reflected this quality, and therefore may have developed a high level of self-confidence within you. However, your parent's high level of self-esteem was no guarantee that you would develop it. But the odd were in your favor. Unfortunately, most of us did not have parents with high self-esteem. I certainly didn't inherit it from either of my parents. Not that they weren't good parents, but because of the way they were raised they did not develop it. And they could only teach what they knew. And when people have low self-esteem they generally overcompensate in some area of their life as a means of coping with it. My father overcompensated his low self-esteem by being a lady's man, also known as a womanizer. I believe he wanted love, but didn't know how to give or receive it, so he substituted sex for it instead. And as the old saying goes, the apple doesn't fall far from the tree, as a young man I followed in his footsteps. I say he wanted love because he seemed to never show it, at least not toward me or in front of me in ways that I understood. And when a boy isn't certain whether his father loves him or not, it creates a void in his heart that causes him to go out and try to fill it with anything that will make him feel accepted. Most often it shows up as seeking the approval of others. I believe my going to college was even an attempt to fill the void of trying to be good enough so that my father would tell me that he was proud of me, and I could equate that with love. But those words never came from his lips. But you know what, I think I'm a better man because of the way he treated our relationship. I became self- sufficient at a relatively young age. I did things that made me feel proud of myself. A wonderful woman, who was emotionally stoic like my dad, came into my life and after a lengthy engagement we got married. And you thought guys only married women that were like their mothers, didn't you?

## I'll Always Love My Mama, She's My Favorite Girl

My mother, bless her heart, is one of the sweetest, gentile, generous person that you ever want to meet. However, she is in need of a spine donor, because she lacks having a backbone. She will do most anything to openly avoid hurting someone's feelings, especially family members. Conflict-avoidance best describes her behavior when an issue ensues that involves the heart. She also overcompensated for her low self-esteem by placing a lot of emphasis on her physical appearance. Which also means that she has a tendency to judge others by their physical appearance. Most of the time when she ridicules or pokes fun at people it's to get a laugh out of you; but I think it also makes her feel like she's a little higher on the appearance totem pole. I recall growing up with the idea that clothes make the man. I used to buy very expensive clothes and shoes, with all the accessories. My appearance was impeccable. Now, I like looking for bargains in thrift stores. Go figure! I inherited both my father's and my mother's low self-esteem traits, and it took me a while before I realized it and began to deal with it. Also, I thought about when I got married and started a family, I would be the example my kids would in all likelihood follow. I began to look at myself as though I was an observer of someone who I was genuinely interested in. And I began to examine what character traits exemplified that of my parents, and how my decisions were affected by these traits. I saw myself as being too critical of myself, and on other people, including my wife, who was passive-aggressive and didn't ever show much of an emotional response. I was very competitive in both my mental and physical endeavors. And I was extremely charismatic, which seem to have given me an edge of likeability, especially when I had to deal with females. There is a verse in the bible that says, "Honor your father and your mother...". This means that to honor someone you endeavor to emulate their character qualities that are deemed honorable, like honesty, courtesy, and generosity. And seek to avoid replicating their character qualities that are flawed. So, if you've carried around the idea that your parents were perfect examples to follow in every way, lose it. They weren't flawless, they were human beings dealing with life challenges as they came. Just keep in mind that you don't always have to be perfect in all of your decision-making in order to be considered a good upstanding human being.

So, as you can see, I had a lot of issues to work through before my self-esteem started to rise like Pillsbury biscuits. Some people surmise that the reason why mental health professionals enter the field is because they have so many personal issues themselves that they need to work out. You know, there may be some truth to that. But the truth is that low self-esteem is what keeps you from living the life that you truly desire, even if you have an abundance of possessions. That only means you have more stuff to try and hide behind. Because the premise behind low self-esteem is that you aren't good enough; and in order for you to compensate for your inadequacies you subjugate yourself by doing things that you think will make you look better and/or feel better, even though it's only a temporary fix.

Low self-esteem can be displayed in many different forms. Renown psychologist Dr. Robert Anthony in his bestselling book, Total Self-Confidence, cites low self-esteem as having major addictive qualities. Know that psychological addictions are more powerful than physical addictions because they go to the root of one's belief system. For example, someone who is addicted to anger may engage in it without consciously knowing that's what they're doing. Their angry reactions to situations may be without provocation from anyone because their instincts have been shaped to view things negatively. Whereas, an alcoholic is conscious of what he is doing and generally acts on taking a drink when he gets a craving.

Here listed are some psychological addictions and behaviors associated with low self-esteem:

- Blaming and Complaining - Instead of acknowledging that you are responsible for your actions, you find it necessary to blame and complain about someone or something that happened to you that you claim causes you to act the way you do. As I mentioned about inheriting my low self-esteem from my parents, I don't blame them. Because I realize they could only teach me what they knew. And what they knew about self-esteem in all probability came from their parents.
- Fault Finding - When you attempt to hide your sense of low self-esteem from others, you find fault with them based on their being in disagreement with you. In other words, you make them out to be wrong because you feel you have to be right. Usually you find fault in other's actions based on the very actions you dislike most about yourself and you resent the idea of letting them get away with it. What you dislike most in others are the faults and weaknesses you have within yourself.
- Need for Attention and Approval - When you feel worthless and think that your thoughts, feelings, and opinions do not matter, you may get a growing compulsion to seek others

continuous attention and approval. It serves as a habitual means to try and minimize the feeling of not being okay. As I mentioned, men and women often use sex as a means of having gained confirmation from someone that they are acceptable, lovable, adorable, charming, and a host of other things that they may otherwise feel deficient about. Sex makes them feel good, and they equate that feeling with the thought that someone thinks they are okay.

- Lack of Close Friends - When you don't like the person that you are, you tend to project that on to others. You go around thinking that they know what you think you know about yourself, and they couldn't possibly want to be a close friend with someone who has all of these faults and flaws. Or, you get into friendships with others and act demanding and overly aggressive and speaking critically and demeaning. All as a means of keeping others at a distance. Distancing oneself from others is interpreted as a means of not letting them find out your dark secrets as to why you dislike being the person that you are.

- Aggressive Need to Win - When you become obsessed with winning for the sake of feeling good about yourself, it generally stems from trying to prove yourself worthy to others. Which is different from being competitive and trying to get the most out of yourself in mastering something you enjoy. Because even if you lose at something, it may disappoint you, but it doesn't affect your self-esteem. This was an area of my transformation in turning my need to win into being competitive for the sake of knowing what I'm capable of doing. I'm a golfer and basketball player, and even though I don't enjoy losing, when it's all said and done, I'm happy just for having competed and done my best.

- Overindulgence - This is probably the behavior where most people with low self-esteem flock to. It is what gives them temporary relief from their feeling of self-rejection. They overindulge in mental and physical opiates that momentarily numbs their emotional pain. Whether it's over-eating, over-drinking, over-spending, over-working, etc. it all boils down to the same thing, people are seeking a temporary solution to an on-going problem. It's no wonder that internet pornography is a multi-billion-dollar industry. It's no wonder gambling casinos are popping up all over the country. It's no wonder the fast-food industry has become the leading source of the American diet. Anne Wilson Schaef's account of this phenomenon of overindulgence that leads to addictions is well portrayed in her book, _When Society Becomes an Addict_. We will talk more about addiction in a subsequent session.

- Depression - This form of low self-esteem occurs when you get totally exasperated with your life because you feel your inadequacy to accomplish the things you want in your life. Sometimes the source is your own expectations, and other times the source may come from the expectations of others. A number of college students come to my office feeling depressed. When we delve into the source of their depression, I found on many occasions that their parent's expectations were the source. Many of the students were in majors they didn't like, and some were at this particular college that they didn't necessarily want to attend, but it was at their parent's insistence. So, if you find yourself feeling depressed, do seek professional help, because it is helpful in navigating you back to the source(s) in order to address it realistically.

- Greed and Selfishness - This aspect of low self-esteem stems from a compulsive need to try and fulfill your every desire by any means necessary. Because you lack self-worth, you over-compensate by becoming self-absorbed with getting what you want, no matter how you get it or who it affects. This type of personality borders on narcissism in that you don't have any interest or concerns about the needs of others. A greedy person feels it is justifiable to take more than their fair share if at all possible.

- Indecision and Procrastination - There are times when we all face indecision when we feel as though we don't have enough information. However, when you have low self-esteem, this can cause you to be immobilized because of an abnormal fear of making a mistake. And not doing the "right" thing can most definitely set you up for ridicule and shame. So, you prefer to do nothing rather than doing something "wrong". The same applies to the procrastinator, as we mentioned earlier, who puts things off for as long as possible for fear of not doing something correct. The perfectionist also falls into this category because he/she has an overwhelming need to present him/herself as perfect. He/she needs to feel above reproach and therefore see themselves better than those who don't meet their criteria for perfection. It's like the parent who tells the child to perform a chore and then goes behind them and does it the "right" way. Perfectionists can frustrate the people around them with their indecisiveness because perfectionists have the desire and the fortitude to overthink almost anything.
- Putting Up a False Front - These are your impressionists. These people will do most anything to appear to be "more" than who they themselves feel they are. They brag and boast about the things they've done and the possessions they have. They mention the "important" people they claim to know. They may be very boisterous and the center of attention in group settings. They display a phony forced laugh when they think it's needed to gain more attention. They are so afraid that others will discover their feeling of inferiority that they are rarely honest about their true feelings to anyone about matters of relevance. Feelings of inferiority are ingrained deeply and usually occur within the first five years of your life. And this feeling is oftentimes reinforced by parents, teachers, religious folk, and anyone who thinks they should have an agenda for you.
- Self-Pity - Have you ever been invited to a pity party. The invitation goes something like this. "I'm having so much trouble in

my life, would you please come and let me tell you all about it". The person throwing the party realizes that you might be inclined to offer them the sympathy they seek for their pathetic life, if they can prove to you that they are not responsible for what is happening to them. Their self-esteem is so low that they have now resorted to deriving pleasure from their pain. They have become so dependent on the sympathy of others that almost anyone can upset them with an unkind word, or facial expression, or comment about their appearance or performance. Many of these "poor me" people not only feel mentally denigrated, but often they are physically incapacitated in some way. When a patient comes to see me for the first time, I let them know that they are given one initial pity party where they can complain about any and everything they wish to complain about. After that I tell them that it's time to go to work on themselves, and they can no longer attribute blame to anyone or any circumstance that is responsible for their current situation. In this way I allow them to vent, but I show them no sympathy. I do empathize with people, especially the ones who struggle with some of the same things I've struggled with. But to sympathize with my patients would only encourage them to continue with their stories of how they are being victimized.

- Divorce - In the case of divorce, either one or both partners may suffer from low self-esteem. This most often occurs when one partner is very dominate and/or controlling which generally intimidates their spouse. When excessive fault-finding is used, it brings into play resentment, deep-seated anger, and bitterness. Under these conditions, both partners may feel inadequate and insecure in their ability to sustain a satisfying marriage, stemming from a desperate need to feel loved. My parents divorced when I was around twenty years old. And according to my observations they didn't have a very loving relationship when they were together. I never saw them kiss or hold hands or say "I love you" to each other. On the other hand, I never heard them argue about anything either. My marriage was pretty much the same, even though mine lasted about ten years longer than my parents. But the biggest difference in our divorces was that mine was by mutual consent, whereas my parents was not. I believe my mom would have stayed in the marriage had my dad been willing to work things out in a reasonable manner. The reason for bringing this up is to let you know, if you don't already know it, that all divorces need not end in bitterness and resentment even if it is present in the marriage. Sometimes putting space between you and your spouse can help you sort things out without the overbearing influence of the other person. I'm not recommending divorce as a solution to your marital problems by no means. *Only* when those problems have reached the proportion of having become irreconcilable differences should you even consider separation or divorce.

- Suicide - A lot of people frown on suicide. Although I do not endorse it, except in extreme cases where the quality of one's life has totally deteriorated, nor do I think that it is a remedy for solving a person's problems. But I do understand that there are things that people struggle with in life that appear to be worse than death. I once saw an episode on the TV program, The Practice, where the defense attorney was defending his client who assisted in a medically induced suicide. The case came down to what was best for the patient who died. The argument was that euthanasia was applicable because the patient was terminal, and most importantly in a lot of physical pain that was beyond management. As a juror, how would you have made the call? Suicide is believed by many to be the highest form of self-hatred. And in most respects, I agree with that. Because there are people who have created a self that they have totally despised and rejected. And some have even cut-off all means of support from those who would have liked to help them. I have treated many people with suicidal tendencies, and the thing they all have in common is their overwhelming desire to get away from themselves. The thing that brings them back is by helping them to realize that they can reconstruct their thoughts about who they see themselves as. And with the proper support, they gradually start breaking down the despicable image they have of themselves when they feel love enter into their space.

So, if any of these behaviors feel familiar to you, then you are in need of a self-esteem boost. Go back to the opening paragraph of this session and re-read it until you get a thorough understanding of what it means. Even if you don't know how to develop and/or use autosuggestions and affirmations at this point which we will get into a little later, stay focused on understanding the fundamentals of faith. Know too that faith is not an intellectual exercise. In fact, your intellect may want to reject the idea that something can exists simply because you are consciously choosing to acknowledge its existence before it is physically manifested. Faith *is* the substance that brings about the manifestation of your thoughts. Just like building a house, you need substances like wood, nails, glue, glass, etc. Well, when pushing a thought to completion or manifestation out into the physical world, it is faith that is the substance. By not allowing your intellect to dictate to you what is possible, you consciously take control of how you choose to think about things. Your intellect is the stepchild of your ego, or the "you" that you want others to think you are. So, your intellect's purpose is to maintain the image of the "self" that your ego created. Which means that the intellect is to reject anything that it cannot comprehend logically or rationally as it has defined logic and reason. But faith is born of the Spirit and resides in the subconscious mind. It does not depend on human reasoning or logic in order to create what it desires. This Spirit is the real YOU. It is the part of you that expresses itself simply as "I AM". Which means self-existent, without dependency on anything. It is this part of you that is fully aware of who you truly are and what it means to be human. A creator within your own beliefs.

# AUTOSUGGESTIONS – AFFIRMING DESIRES

**AUTO-SUGGESTIONS** - HILL defines this as "the agency of communication between that part of the mind where conscious thought takes place, and that which serves as the seat of action for the subconscious mind." In other words, it's like the conduit for turning thoughts into action. The type of thoughts that you give continuous attention to that interplays with the subconscious mind which in turn acts on them. Hypnotherapy uses a similar method of the power of suggestion to get at unconscious or repressed memories that may be significantly affecting a person's behaviors. Similarly, you can use this power of suggestion to command your subconscious to fulfill your desires. Since the subconscious mind is impartial as to what desires you want to fulfill, your focused thoughts must becomes specific as to what it is that you want, coupled with an emotional attachment to your desires; and having faith in the subconscious' ability to perform its duty. The subconscious mind is open to every serious suggestion it is given. And repeated messages tend to take hold when the level of desire rises above the threshold of unbelievability to possibility. The subconscious mind is the power that makes real that which your senses perceive as your reality. Hill says that, "Your ability to use the principle of autosuggestion will depend, very largely, upon your capacity to concentrate upon a given desire until that desire becomes a burning obsession.". The autosuggestions and repetitive affirmations serve as a means of intensifying the emotions (feelings) of your desires, which convinces the subconscious to act upon it. It is the feeling aspect of your thoughts that give vitality, life, and action to your desires.

Autosuggestions are basically messages that you have preprogrammed your mind to accept through repetition that becomes activated when you're in a situation that the mind responds to by projecting a specific behavior. These autosuggestions can also be used in completely new situations that allows you to describe yourself according to your desired outcome; or they can be used in familiar situations where you have previously shown yourself to exert effective behaviors. In other words, if some situation did not result in the way you expected, you don't have to autosuggest that you are to blame. You can suggest to yourself that this was a learning experience that will help you conduct yourself differently when a similar situation arises. So, your description of yourself can be that of a student learning in the classroom of life, rather than an idiot who made a big mistake.

## +'s and −'s

Autosuggestions work both positively and negatively. The negative aspect occurs when you've done something that you perceive as having gone contrary to your logical rational. And you automatically respond by saying something like, "I'm so stupid", or "Why do I keep doing dumb stuff?". At this point, you may think that you have said these things in response to the event. But, in actuality, the event came after the autosuggestion. Because you had to have already had the autosuggestion that you are stupid or that you always do stupid stuff embedded in your mind in order to say those words at the conclusion of the event. Because if you didn't have those autosuggestions lodged in your mind, you couldn't respond with those words. If an error occurs you might say, "Oops, or Oh my", but not something that is demeaning if you didn't feel that way about yourself. So, the connection between the events in your life and your responses to them are determined by the autosuggestions that you have accepted about yourself. In other words, the words you use as a descriptive of yourself in any event is a direct reflection of your self-perception, the event merely validates or mirrors that perception. Thoughts always precedes actions, whether the thoughts are conscious or unconscious. Sometimes the autosuggestion builds over time and the event that reflects it may be years in the making, depending on how frequent the thought is entertained. But sometimes, the event that mirrors the autosuggestion can occur in the blink of an eye. Like when a person does physical harm to another person in a fit of jealous rage. Or when a person gets a sudden urge and says something meaningful to another person that helps them get through a crisis.

Autosuggestion's were a part of ancient tribal rituals when someone was to perform a very challenging act. The suggestion would be given to him by the tribal leader, and the adherent would then be surrounded by tribe members in chants and dancing. It was believed that the Great Spirit was being called upon to give the person courage and a vision for success. But the premise was based on the drum beat and the dance to elevate the vibration from the lower fear level to a higher fearless level. Oftentimes, the person went into a trancelike state when the ritual was performed. Well, I'm not recommending that you seek out a medicine man, guru, or witch doctor to access autosuggestions that could benefit you. I mention this for the purpose of letting you know that autosuggestions are nothing new; and that they must be used in conjunction with a means that elevates them in your belief from an "I can't" to an "I can".

The following poem describes the phenomenon of the law of autosuggestions when they permeate thoughts:

"If you *think* you are beaten, you are,
If you *think* you dare not, you don't.
If you like to win, but you *think* you can't,
It is almost certain you won't.

"If you *think* you'll lose, you're lost,
For out in the world we find,
Success begins with a fellow's will
It's all in the *state of mind*.

"If you *think* you are outclassed, you are,
You've got to *think* high to rise,
You've got to *be sure of yourself* before
You can ever win a prize.

"Life's battles don't always go
To the stronger or faster man,
But soon or late the man who wins
Is the man WHO THINKS HE CAN!"

There is a distinct difference between making a declaratory state-ment, or autosuggestion, and "Magical thinking", or leaving things up to chance. There is an old Chinese Proverb that says, "The journey of a thousand kilometers begins with the first step". But even before you take that first step you must recognize where you are in order to know where you're going. There is something else that is important to know as you start your trek, and that is, you must be willing to ac-cept life on Its terms and how it shows up all around you. That's not to say that you can't change what you see. It is to say that what you see is what you get to respond to. It isn't a matter of what you are con-fronted with in life, but it does matter what your response to it is. In working with people, one of the biggest obstacles I found that gets in the way of happiness, is constant complaining about mishaps. Guess what? Everyone has them. No one goes through life unscathed from events that challenges their ability to face it. Because your character is forged in the crucible of your mishaps. So, as you begin your sojourn down the "yellow brick road" of life, as did Dorothy in the movie, The Wizard of Oz, keep in mind that there will come a time when you will be assailed metaphorically by witches, flying monkeys, and other assailants that will make attempts to thwart you from completing your journey. But, know too, there are forces at work that will help guide you as to what to do in these circumstances. And, remember, like Dorothy, that your goal is to get home. And home is the place where you come to know yourself for who you truly are and experience the joy and happiness that life seeks to give you. And there truly is no place like home.

## Play it again, Sam!

Many of our thoughts are like records that are played over and over again because we like the way they sound. Those thoughts usually give you the feeling that you are "right" about something. And we all like to be right, right? So, when it comes to changing your behavior, you must give up the thought of being "right" in the area you would like to change. For instance, if you're not a millionaire, and you want to become a millionaire, then how you presently think about how to become a millionaire must not be right, because you're not. So, somewhere lodged in your mind is a suggestion that states, "I don't know how to become a millionaire". But, if you hold to that suggestion, then you're unlikely to become a millionaire. However, if you want to change your behavior, you must change your thought about being right about not knowing how to be something you want to become. Which means that you must replace that thought with one that states, "I know how to become a millionaire". Right? Right! That's why you are reading this book, to reinforce your autosuggestions that support you in making changes in your life. So, what you are doing is like the tribal ritual we talked about earlier. You're raising your inner vibrations to a level that supports your affirmations.

Autosuggestions can be used both positively and negatively as indicated in the poem previous quoted. Many are used to support unhealthy habits or addictions. Some autosuggestions may have gained entrance into your thinking from significant people in our lives because you are prone to believe them, that's why you consider them significant. This usually occurs at an early age between a child and the authority figures that child interacts with. I recall when I was growing up there was a boy in my neighborhood who came from what was then described as a broken home, meaning his mother and father were divorced. He lived with his mother, who seemed to be bitter and carried a lot of resentment toward her ex-husband. So, whenever she got mad at her son, she would spew out the phrase, "You're just like your no-good daddy!" Well, after being told that a number of times you can only image the indelible imprint it made in his mind about who he was. And as it turned out, when he got older, he ended up getting into trouble with the authorities. All because he developed an inferiority complex based on his mother's suggestions that became his autosuggestions about who he perceived himself as being. I can only imagine how many times that tape of "You're just like your no-good daddy" played in his head whenever he felt inadequate. As you can see, it is what you tell yourself about yourself, particularly in times of emotional upheaval that determines what outcome you'll experience. When your affirmations, or self-talk, turns into autosuggestions, they will help you maintain your focus on striving forward to fulfill the desires of your heart.

I have listed some positive affirmation in **Appendix C** taken from Dr. Robert Anthony's book, Total Self-Confidence, with some modifications. These are only examples, feel free to state your own as they apply to your particular situation.

# SPECIALIZED KNOWLEDGE – CONCENTRATED FOCUS

SPECIALIZED KNOWLEDGE IS the knowledge that directs your attention toward a particular result. It is the knowledge that knows what needs to be done, and how to get it done. But first, you must decide on what type of specialized knowledge you'll need in order to live abundantly. Your purpose in life should provide you with clues as to what it is you like to do as a means of fulfilling your life's goal. You then must gather accurate information from dependable sources to acquire this knowledge. Hill says the more important sources are:

a) One's own experience and education.
b) Experience and education available through cooperation of others
c) Colleges and Universities.
d) Public libraries
e) Special training courses, such as satellite schools and home study courses

What Hill didn't know at the time of his writing, is that the internet is now the most prominent source for gaining information on any topic. These other sources are not useless, however, they simple pale in comparison to the information that you can receive on-line in a moment's notice. But, because there is so much information on the internet to be had, you must be willing and able to learn the difference between reliable and unreliable sources. You may have to cross-reference data from several sources in order to determine exactly what you'll need. Because specialized knowledge is specifically designed to be organized and structured toward the implementation of practical plans that will bring a desired result. Also, it can prove to be extremely helpful if the people you associate with when you begin to administer your plan of action, are knowledgeable about success and/or offer you encouragement to be successful. Because if you need an answer to some question that arises that should be addressed, knowing someone who is acquainted with success may provide you with the answer you need.

Colleges, universities, and trade schools all teach you how to acquire specialized knowledge, and so does the school of life. Many inventors and innovators developed their specialize knowledge from the school of life by noticing what was needed in their environment to improve conditions. And even when you are presented with the same concepts and ideas as others, it is up to you to make it your own by tailoring it according to your desires. For example, you can have a degree in business administration as does someone else, but the person who uses their business knowledge as a self-expression of specific desires they want manifested in their life will experience a great deal more success. That's taking specific knowledge and specializing it to suit your unique expression of it. I stated earlier that the difference between abundance and scarcity is understanding. This is where specialized knowledge plays a role. It's taking information and knowing how to use it in such a way that multiplies the results.

## The Slothful Servant

There is a story in the Christian bible that talks about a master going on a business trip and leaving three of his servants with varying amounts of money to invest for him. When the master returns, the servant whom he gave let's call it, $500.00, doubled his money. And the master was very pleased with the servant for his diligence. Then the master called in another servant whom he had given $200.00, and he also doubled the money that was given to him. And again, the master was pleased with this servant for being so dutiful. But the third servant who was given $100.00 had done nothing with the money that was given to him. When asked by his master as to why he had done nothing with the money that was given to him, his reply was blaming his master for being an austere man, and that he was afraid that if he had lost the money on a poor investment the master would be livid and possibly take his anger out on him. The master responded by saying that he could have at least put the money in the bank where it would have drawn some interest. The master was not pleased with the servant and called him lazy because of his lack of enthusiasm. This is an allegory. The master represents desire. The money represents knowledge, everybody is given some. The investing of the money represents the imagination. When your imagination takes the knowledge that comes from your desires, it manifests, or multiplies the results according to your diligence to maintain focus. So, having knowledge without the use of your imagination will not manifest your desire. Knowledge is useless *unless* it manifests a desired result.

## And the Difference would be?

All knowledge is based on information, but not all information leads to knowledge. With the proliferation of information one can get via the internet and television, there appears to be widespread knowledge on any and every subject imaginable. However, all of the information you can glean from the internet or television news may not necessarily be as reliable as you might think, nor useful in helping you gain a fuller understanding of something you're seeking to know. That's why the emphasis is placed on the acquisition of specialized knowledge versus general information. And with all that juicy information running around out there, it's easy to get distracted from collecting information that can be used in a specialized way. So, the question to ask yourself periodically as you are rummaging through the various sources of knowledge is, "How useful is this information in helping me to fulfill my desire?". Some desires you have may be frivolous, like wanting to know the baseball score of your favorite team after the game has been played without you having viewed it. Other desires are tantamount in terms of you needing to know something that will affect how you will make an important decision. Such as the history of a particular stock that you are considering investing a substantial amount of money in. That's why it becomes important to write down your goals and objectives, and periodically reading them and see how you're progressing. That way you can remain focused on what you need to do, and not clutter up your mind with a lot of useless information. Frivolity, like fantasy is okay as long as you can separate it from important aspects of your reality. Life should not be taken so seriously that you can't digress into thoughts that stray away from things you're subject to do versus things you may never do. Like winning the lottery and buying your own remote island and turning it into a resort. But, trying to live your life in a fantasy world will not satisfy your deep longing for expressing yourself in a manner that reflects your highest potential.

## Why Can't You Be Like Everyone Else?

Believe it or not, most people are trying to be like everyone else. Whether you call it blending into society or maintaining the status quo, it all boils down to not trying to be a standout among people. And conformity is the most profound autosuggestion given to people in all societies. On the surface, conformity appears to be something needful in all societies in order to maintain civility and common ideologies that support the masses ability to live a fundamentally peaceful existence. However, when societies use conformity to pigeonhole people in a class system where they are bound in impoverished conditions, then conformity is not something that is to be valued. Even societies that use socioeconomic status to perpetuate the idea that there is not enough room "at the top" for everyone. So, the prevailing suggestion for those who are not in the upper echelon of society is to conform to your relegated lower-class status. Which in most instances turns conformity into complacency and/or a mediocre attitude about your ability to attain the life you truly desire. And once you have accepted your "place" in society then it may feel very natural to live within the confines of its limitations.

How frequent you make conscious concerted efforts to give yourself affirmations regarding your ability to attain your highest desires will determine the rapidity and quality of your ascent to your personal success. That statement sounds frightening to people who have accepted mediocrity as the norm for their life. One of the most prolific metaphysicians of our time, Marianne Williamson describes this fearful feeling in her book, A Return to Love, and it is worth quoting here in its entirety, she says, *"Our deepest fear is not that we are inadequate. Our deepest fear is that we are powerful beyond measure. It is our light, not our darkness that most frightens us. We ask ourselves, 'Who am I to be brilliant, gorgeous, talented, fabulous? Actually, who are you not to be? You are a child of God. Your playing small does not serve the world. There is nothing enlightening about shrinking so that other people won't feel insecure around you. We are all meant to shine, as children do. We were born to make manifest the glory of God that is within us. It's not just in some of us; it's in everyone. And as we let our own light shine, we unconsciously give other people permission to do the same."* What she's saying is that if we are to conform, let it be for the highest good. Let's conform to the idea that we are more than what we may appear to be, and therefore will not settle for a lower opinion of ourselves by anyone, including ourselves. As my grandmother would say, "I may not be what I want to be but thank God I'm not what I use to be!".

The acquisition of specialized knowledge is not difficult when you are motivated. So, my suggestion for you is to pay attention to your environment and things that you find an interest in, then treat it like a hobby. Pursue that interest with whatever amount of time and energy that you can give it. Allow your imagination to conjure up ways that this new "hobby" may become profitable. This is where specialized knowledge comes in, once you have determined what it may take for you to know how to bring your idea into fruition. You may need a coach or a tutor, or someone who will help keep you accountable for the completion of the steps needed to start and complete your idea. Your ability to stay motivated will come from you envisioning yourself as already completed what you have set out to accomplish. In other words, you are moving from the end goal to the present. Your mind serves as a magnet guiding you forward toward what you have pictured your desired experience to be. If you want to be an author, then picture yourself as having already completed your book, I did. Imagine what it would feel like to see your book on the shelf at your favorite bookstore, or on your website, or when you click on Amazon books. The specialized knowledge you acquire will give you the confidence to realize that your dream cannot remain a dream. Because for you, your dream will come true.

# IMAGINATION – THE ARCHITECT OF DREAMS

HILL DESCRIBES THE imagination as the "workshop" of the mind. It is where impulses, ideas, and desires are given shape, form and action. He goes on to say that the imaginative faculty functions in two ways. One is called *synthetic imagination* which uses old concepts, ideas, and plans and rearranges them into new combinations. In other words, it basically works with material already in existence obtained either through past experiences, education, or observations. The other faculty of imagination is called, *creative imagination*, which places the finite mind of man in direct contact with Infinite Intelligence. This faculty of the imagination is where man receives inspiration, insight, intuitive hunches, and new ideas. And because it connects the conscious mind with the subconscious mind, one man can resonate with the subconscious mind of another man. The creative imagination works automatically and is especially active when man is stimulated by a strong desire. Hill says, "Desire is only a thought, an impulse. It is nebulous and ephemeral. It is abstract, and of no value, until it has been transformed into its physical counterpart." Thus, it is your imagination that carries your desires into its workshop and fashions it according to what it knows is possible.

## It Was Just My Imagination Running Away With Me!

Everything that you ever have or ever will encounter starts from a thought that developed into an idea that formulates a plan that caused certain actions that are performed. These actions are the constructs of your imagination. Whether you are using your imagination consciously or not, its primary function is to provide you with a plan of action suited to your situation. As was mentioned previously, the imagination is heavily influenced by the autosuggestions that you have placed in your mind that represents your deep-seated thoughts you have about yourself. Unlike your conscious mind that frames and categorizes all of your knowledge into what it perceives as logical and reasonable definitions, the imagination is not restricted to utilize the processes you call reason and logic, or even that which you may have dubbed as unreasonable and illogical. In fact, the imagination is most effective when it is allowed to move freely, or as some people might say, when it is used to think outside the box. The box being your current frame of mind. The imagination is also impartial in that it doesn't recognize the labels you attach to your experiences. In other words, to the imagination an experience is just an experience, neither good, bad, or indifferent.

The transformation of your thoughts into an action plan as constructed by your imagination can either work against your desires or for them. Say for instance, you want to be in a new relationship. If you carry the thought that you will be rejected if you approach someone you're interested in, then you have virtually instructed your imagination to construct a scenario that will include the experience of rejection. If on the other hand, you think that the person you're interested in will be receptive to your advances, then you will have instructed your imagination to construct a scenario that includes acceptance. That's not to say that you necessarily have control over the other person. But it is to say that because your imagination is rooted in your subconscious that you have the capability of resonating with the other person according to your own desire. Remember, there is only one Infinite Intelligence and everyone's subconscious mind is intricately linked to it. That's what gives you the ability to connect with others. It's like being on the internet where millions of other computers are connected, but each one decides what they want to access. And through this network, people on computers can communicate with one another. The spiritual network works in the same way. However, it operates on vibrations. You may have heard someone use the expression, "she's giving off a bad vibe". What's being expressed is that she does not want to be bothered, and the person who feels her vibration knows it without her having to express it in words.

## What If...

When it comes to the use of the imagination, I recall an incident when I was in graduate school. I would drive down from my home in the Napa Valley to Berkeley. My good friend, Morris (Mo) Brown rode down with me, though we did not attend the same school, he would catch the Bart train from Berkeley to San Francisco where he was attending school. I remember him making the comment about buying a lottery ticket, and my response to him was that his odds of winning was very low. He went on to remark that he didn't buy the ticket expecting to win, but rather to ignite his imagination about what he would do with the money. He said having the fantasy was worth far more than the $1 he spent for the ticket. Which makes sense if you don't think about having a lot of money any other way. And I imagine many people who buy lottery tickets buy them for that very same reason. Quite a revelation. And quite a lesson about the power of our imagination, which we certainly need in order to obtain riches. And we don't have to spend a dollar to use it. Supposing however that you use your imagination to create your reality rather than a fantasy. Say for instance, you do decide to become a millionaire. It wouldn't matter if you won the lottery or not. And in all probability, you probably won't. But, that's not to say that the use of your imagination cannot create a viable means for you to become rich. However, there are other factors that should be taken into consideration when making a decision about the lifestyle you want to have and how money fits into the equation. Yes, money will be a part of it, but other factors may include moral or ethical decisions about the duties you perform. Perhaps time constraints may be of a concern regarding time spent away from home. Or there may be human rights issues and/or health care concerns that needs to be addressed. In other words, money shouldn't be regarded as the end-all be-all that pertains to living a satisfying lifestyle. The pursuit of money is prevalent within the U.S. economy because the survival of capitalism depends on it. And, as you learned from Economics 101, the problem occurs in capitalism when there is a large discrepancy between supply and demand. But, what does any of this have to do with wanting to be a millionaire? you ask. Well, it means that you will need to be conscious of the climate you are creating on your quest to riches. By that I mean, you must not compromise who you are and what you believe your purpose to be for the sake of living abundantly. I think being rich is a good thing. In fact, I wish more *good* people were rich. By good people, I mean people who believe in trying to make this world a better place to live for everyone.

## Imagine That!

It is my approach to most writings that have been proclaimed as sacred to look for the psychological content. The reason for my doing so is because life as we know it is not merely the existence of physical matter; but rather unseen forces of energy that created and continues to create the physical world. Therefore, these sacred writings I feel must address the interplay between the visible and the invisible. Many sacred writings allude to an unseen God. But, in order to know of the unseen God, one must use their mind to form the basis for something that exists that has no physical form. So, it stands to reason that sacred writings must use symbology to convey the concept of a deity since there would be no other means to write about something abstract in a concrete manner. This was emphasized to me from the works of Neville Goddard in his collection of writings on the Power of Imagination. He speaks of the symbolism of the Christian bible as a means to enlighten those who use their intellect and intuition to understand the connection between reality and consciousness. If, as Neville postulates, consciousness is the only reality, then man's consciousness must have created the world in which he dwells. But he is also clear that man's consciousness is not devised by man, but rather by an Infinite Intelligence that exists within the mind of all men. The key is to access It through the denial of the perceptions of the senses when they run counter with your noblest desires. Because it is Infinite Intelligence's Nature to express Its noblest characteristics as You.

The use of your imagination ties into this whole concept of how things are revealed to you. Because without the imagination you could not believe that anything was possible. It is your imagination that helps you to reconstruct the interpretations you have previously placed on an experience you had and look at it from a totally different perspective. I recall my ex-wife telling me of a woman at her church who told her how sorry she was that my ex-wife had a failed marriage. I explained to my ex-wife that she should not allow anyone else to define what her experiences are because their interpretations are usually not accurate. Their preconceived ideas about someone else's experiences are simply unfounded because they were not present and do not have all of the facts, including the feelings she may have been experiencing at the time. I went on to tell her that she did not have to interpret a divorce as a failed marriage, and I gave her ample reasons why. She began to see that she did not have a failed marriage, but merely one that ended. No different than when someone retires from a job. They didn't necessarily have a failed career, they simply had one they chose to end. And not that a marriage and a job are the same type of relationships; but the events that occur in both are interpreted in the same manner, based on how you perceived you were affected. That's what imagination does for you. It helps you to look past what may appear to be something, when it may totally be something else. That's why we are admonished to judge not by appearances. If you've ever been to a magic show and have seen the magician saw the lady in half, and she lived, then you know what I'm speaking of.

## Fairytales do come true, It can happen to You

All of your fantasies are rooted in your imagination. But not all imaginings are fantasized. In psychological terms, the word fantasy means a thought or idea not rooted in reality. In other words, the likelihood of the fantasy occurring is highly improbable. However, a long-held fantasy can create the illusion of reality. When I was a boy, there was a man in my neighborhood who I presumed wanted to be recognized for his intelligence. He fabricated stories about how college professors acknowledged his wisdom, and he claimed to have read 100 books a year. I had heard him tell these stories so many times, that I became convinced that he came to believe they were true. Even though the accounts of his stories were void of any evidence, he probably could pass a polygraph test based on his believability. As you can see, the imagination has the power to create a fantasy world, if you like living in one, or it can create a world of reality. The only difference is, the reality world that the imagination creates requires you to put those thoughts and ideas into action and not just into words. In fact, when it gives you an idea of what's possible for you to achieve a desire that you have, it's best not to say too much about it. Because you'll find yourself spending most of your time and energy talking about it rather than doing what's needful to move forward. You end up settling for the secondary gain of believing that the people you are talking to are interested in what you say you are going to do. And just because you can convince others that you are going to do something, does not get the job done. I recall when I started writing this book, I had to stop talking about writing this book so that I could start writing the book. If you must talk about your ideas for accomplishing something, do so with someone who supports you fully and can offer you suggestions as to how to go about doing something that will help your process of bringing your idea to life.

Keep in mind that your imagination doesn't know the difference between fact and fiction. It operates on your desires both conscious and subconscious. Which means you can consciously override the desires of your subconscious mind, even if it's only temporary. Say for instance, your subconscious mind uses your imagination to create a condition for you to be very helpful in that situation. But, upon entering the situation, you encounter a person who had offended you in a previously encounter. And let's say you haven't reached the point of having shown forgiveness toward this person for having mistreated you. You feel you have every justification for not being of assistance because this person doesn't deserve it. Now, you can continue to do what you were first inclined to do and be helpful in that situation, or you can override it consciously and squander an opportunity to express a part of you that desires to show mercy. But just because you overturned the decision to do the "right" thing, doesn't mean that you will not encounter a similar situation, however the next time it just might be you who finds yourself in need of help rather than giving it. "Blessed are the merciful, for they shall obtain mercy".

## My Imaginary Friend

Perhaps when you were a child you created an imaginary friend, or perhaps not. Usually children who are either an only child, or a child who doesn't have a sibling near in age to them, create such imaginary playmates. But creating an imaginary friend is not limited to children in these conditions, because a child's mind is active and their greatest desire is to have fun interacting with others, even if they have to make them up. The world of make-believe is a child's playground. Their playmate(s) can be either animate or inanimate. The animate objects can be a stuffed toy, like a teddy bear, or a doll, or even a pet. The inanimate is the person they carry around in their head that they have conversations with usually when others aren't around. These imaginary friends serve not only the purpose of entertaining the child, but also as their main confidant. It's the child's way of using his or her imagination to help them talk about things that they care about. And perhaps to have a dialog with someone they feel will provide them with an answer to some things they don't fully understand, even if the answer isn't accurate. It's the comfort the child receives from having someone on their level to talk with. A child's imaginary friend may also help them to feel safe and comforted when they are in a dysfunctional relationship with their caregivers. And most importantly the imaginary friend may help the child realize that they have someone that is always interested in talking about and doing whatever it is they want to talk about or do. To the child, this imaginary friend's friendship is as real as the clothes they put on their body.

Perhaps it may be time for you to revisit your childhood and establish a relationship with an imaginary friend or two who may provide you with some of these same qualities. Some of you may already have an imaginary friend, you may refer to as God, Jesus, Buddha, Allah, or some other name. You may be tempted to discount the idea that your belief in a deity is something other than your imaginary friend, but in effect, it is. Because it only exists in your imagination. Where else could it exist? You cannot provide proof of its existence, nor can anyone else provide you with proof. And by proof, I mean physical evidence. But this does not mean that because something cannot be proven with empirical evidence that it doesn't exist. As a matter of fact, it is the absence of physical proof that makes it that much more personal to you. What I'm pointing out is that because the idea of a deity exist in your imagination is what makes it real to you. If you believe in a Higher Power, then wouldn't it make sense that the Higher Power would use something that would make Its existence seem real to you? In other words, there has to be some mechanism by which things from the inanimate realm can reveal things to you in the animate world. That mechanism is your imagination. Whenever a supreme idea comes to mind, it is your imagination that helps you to see the magnitude of that idea. Whenever you get a glimmer of hope when faced with a difficult situation, it is your imagination that increases your faith and gives you the assurance that things will turn out alright. Whenever you are assailed by doubts and fears, it is your imagination that shines its light of truth that guilds you to calmness and the feeling of safety. And whenever you desire to express a higher and nobler version of yourself, it is your imagination that sets the course for your actions. You see, your imagination is your friend and servant that wants to talk about and do whatever it is you want to talk about and do. Metaphorically, your imagination is the virgin, impregnated by a thought, that gives birth to the holy child of a desire fulfilled.

Mr. Hill used his imagination in this way to create the Master Mind concept with people he admired and studied. When he was reshaping his thinking about himself, he felt it was necessary to use autosuggestion as a way of imprinting certain thoughts into his mind. So, he employed the technique of holding what he called council meetings with nine imaginary friends who he referred to as his "invisible counselors". He would tell them specifically what he desired to acquire from them based on what he knew about their character. He stated that these cabinet meetings felt very real to him even though he knew consciously they were just in his imagination. He concluded that what he gained from his meetings with these invisible counselors was that they took him into "glorious paths of adventure, (they) rekindled an appreciation of true greatness, encouraged creative endeavor, and emboldened the expression of honest thought". Emulating someone who you consider admirable is the part of life that helps bring out the best in you. No different from holding disdain for someone who brings out the worst in you. By beholding you become changed.

# ORGANIZED PLANNING – PUTTING DESIRE INTO ACTION

ORGANIZED PLANNING IS the part of the process that puts the meat on the skeleton, or framework, that your imagination devised. It is the actual blueprint of what it is that will get accomplished in order for you to realize your desired result of a specified sum of money, or any other thing you wish to achieve. Since there is no such thing as getting something for nothing, this is the something that you are committing to in order to bring about the desired results. And in order for this plan to survive, you must take the leadership role in overseeing every aspect and detail of its development. Mr. Hill suggests that you develop what he calls a "Master Mind". This is a support group of people who have experience, education, and expertise in areas that you perhaps don't. They don't necessarily have to be in your field, but they are there to offer you sound advice from a perspective of having known some measure of success themselves. In today's fast pace market with countless people who consult in almost every area of commerce and services, you may not need a whole team of people. But you probably will need someone to consult with from time to time who may offer you suggestions and ask appropriate questions along the way. It would be someone like a therapist, a life coach, a mentor, or anyone who has your best interest at heart. I believe It makes you more accountable when you know there is someone who is acquainted with what you're doing and tracking your progress. Since you are the CEO of this organized plan for your life, I will offer the following attributes of leadership Mr. Hill states as qualifiers.

1. Unwavering courage in your exercise of the knowledge you have about your occupation, and the confidence you have within yourself.
2. Self-control over your emotions so that they don't interfere with your ability to move forward.
3. A keen sense of justice so that you can recognize if a situation that you created is fair for everyone involved.
4. Definiteness of decision based on your ability to analyze a situation and stick by a decision because you believe it to be the best decision possible for that particular situation.
5. Definiteness of plans based on your ability to plan your work and work your plan. This aspect is the basis and guiding force for all of your accomplishments.
6. The habit of doing more than paid for. Develop the attitude of doing whatever it takes to accomplish your plan of action. Even when you may have thought that you had some help available in doing a particular phase of your plan. If it's not there, then you do it until you can get help, if needed.
7. A pleasing personality goes a long way in soliciting help from those who can give it. Very few people acquire massive fortunes by themselves. They get help sometimes in unexpected places from people who are attracted to them simply because they have a pleasing personality.
8. Sympathy and understanding are the basis for connecting with people who need to know from your actions that you care about them. And the more you are willing to understand them and the unique person that they are, the greater the connection.
9. Mastery of details involves knowing how to perform your duties and knowing how to delegate those duties that are not

within the scope of leadership. A strong leader does not perform all of the detailed work; but the leader knows all the details of what needs to be done and how to get it done.

10. <u>Willingness to assume full responsibility</u> means that "the buck stops here!". No matter what goes awry in your plan, nobody or no circumstance stands to blame. When you assume full responsibility, it means that you must find out what was the cause of something happening that was not according to plan and fixing it. You go under the assumption that if something goes awry it is because you hadn't accounted for it, even if it was something unforeseen.

11. <u>Cooperation</u> means that the successful leader knows how to incorporate the assistance of others by showing them the same level of respect that he/she commands. A tyrannical leader may get others to comply with their demands with threats and manipulative tactics, but they will not have their cooperation. Because cooperation means working together for the same cause toward the same objective.

So, as you begin to think about developing an organized plan, jot down some ideas as to what you think will be required for you to pull it off. With a little bit of research, you might discover that it's not as difficult as it once seemed. You may need to further your education either in a classroom, or on your computer with on-line correspondence classes, or OJT, on-the-job-training through some type of apprenticeship, or reading books on the subject matter you are interested in. Whether you're looking to apply for a new job or thinking about creating a new one. Or maybe you have an idea for promoting a product or inventing one. Or perhaps there's a service industry that you've thought about getting into but didn't have the motivation until now to pursue it. Take notes because these notes will develop into a plan of action, without them you're just spinning ideas. The writing of this book came from my notes that are scribbled in five legal note pads that started over ten years ago. Whenever I came up with an idea, I'd write it down. I keep a notepad by my bed, and one in my car. But, I'm old-school. Today, you can talk into your phone and dictate a message as ideas come to you. But, at some point you will still need to transcribe it either on paper or in some word-processing program on your computer. The point is, you have to start somewhere, sometime, and the best place to start is right where you are, and the best time to start is right NOW!

## In Search of a Tony Robbins?

Is motivational speaking a lost art? We don't seem to have as many national motivational speakers around as we once had. Speakers like Tony Robbins, Deepak Chopra, Les Brown, and Wayne Dyer are a dying breed of speakers who inspired millions of people to take control of their lives through their television appearances, books, and seminars. They did this because they understood that most people lack inspiration and are not shown appreciated for who they are, and they cared enough to provide instructions for them. But there are still motivational speakers out there, and many of them are everyday people who go about their work with exuberance and enthusiasm that sets them apart as true "heroes and heroines". You can see some of them as they tell their stories on Ted TV or on YouTube. Motivation in and of itself is not the problem most people have. Because no matter what you do, you do because you are motivated. Which simply means that you choose to do one thing over another, for whatever reason you make the choice. So, if you decide to sing in the shower, you will do so because you're motivated by a desire to sing. This is more like a general motivation. It's the type of motivation that's associated with an event that bring about a certain feeling and requires little to no outside inspiration to be acted upon. Then there is what you might call negative motivation. This is the motivation that is nonproductive but is relied upon for its secondary benefit. For instance, a person who constantly complains to others about some ailment they suffer with. The complaining is negative and non-productive, but the motivation is for sympathy from the person they're complaining to. But what kind of motivation do you need when you're choosing to tackle a task that involves an intense concerted effort to maintain your focus on completing it. That type of motivation requires an _association_ of the thing you want to accomplish with the purpose you see for your life. And that's primarily because without an aim, you drift mindlessly from one thing to another routinely. Like the old saying goes, "If you don't know where you're going, any old road will take you there.".

So, in order for you to put your desires into action, it requires that you set your mental compass toward an aim that is personal to you. This may require you to do a little brainstorming with yourself or a person who knows you well. And don't dismiss a thought simply because you think it may sound ridiculous to others. Some of the greatest ideas were brought into being because the person chose not to allow popular opinions to sway their decision. And the first line of questioning begins with, "What is it that I really want?", and "Am I willing to pay the price for it?". When you've done that, then you start the process of putting your desires into action by thinking from that viewpoint that you have set for yourself. Note carefully that I did not say that you are to merely think about what it is you want, I said that you must think _from_ that mental position. In other words, this is where you use your imagination to create the feeling of already having accomplished what you set out to do and allow that feeling to be your motivating force. Because motivation is a feeling to do something you feel like doing. This type of motivation brings into play what is called the law of assumption. I alluded to this law previously, but I now offer you a quote from the person who perhaps may have formalized the concept of this law. That person is Neville Goddard, and here is what he states about the law of assumption. "Each assumption has it's corresponding world. If you are truly observant you will notice the power of your assumptions to change circumstances which appear wholly immutable. You, by your conscious assumptions determine the nature of the world in which you live. Ignore the present state and assume the wish fulfilled. Claim it; *it will respond.* The law of assumption is the means by which the fulfillment of your desires may be realized. Every moment of your life, *consciously or unconsciously*, you are assuming a feeling. You can no more avoid assuming a feeling than you can avoid eating and drinking. All you can do is control the nature of your assumptions. Thus, it is clearly seen that the control of your assumptions is the key you now hold to an ever expanding, happier, more noble life.". In essence, you generate the feeling of having accomplished your desire by assuming that it has already occurred for you.

## Oops, I Did It Again!

Success and failure are simply labels' people attach to things that do or do not measure up to some standard they have established. And even though these standards may be arbitrary and self-imposed, they may not always offer the individual the most accurate analysis of an achievement or lack thereof. The label success is sometimes dangled in front of people like a carrot on a stick in front of the donkey that can never reach. And in their frustration and many disappointments, they oftentimes give up. The word failure is frightening to some people. Because they associate failure with the idea that something must be wrong with them if they don't succeed. But, the only thing "wrong" with them is that they don't desire what they claim to want bad enough. Which means that they don't apply sufficient discipline to see their dreams come to fruition. I teach a class in psychopathology, and I tell my students that the main objective of school is to teach them how to become disciplined, especially if they didn't learn it at home. Exercising discipline is the cornerstone of organized planning and honing your skills. Some people are naturals at certain things, like sports, or art, or music. But even gifted athletes practice rigorously to stay in shape and elevate their skill level. Gifted artist may work for days or weeks or years on a piece of art that they envision in their mind. It took Michelangelo almost four years to complete painting the ceiling of the Sistine Chapel in Vatican City. No one can make a claim of having succeeded in accomplishing something that required time and energy without exercising discipline. There is an admonition in the Christian bible that says, "Teach discipline to a child while he is young, and when he is old, he will not depart from it".

## Are You sure Beethoven got Started this Way?

While growing up, I heard the statement, practice makes perfect, quite often when I was taking piano lessons. I wasn't very fond of having to practice the piano at home an hour each day because it cut into my playtime with my friends after school. However, at some level in my thoughts, I knew that I would not be able to play my recital pieces mistake free if I didn't practice. Even though practicing sucked. But I did enjoy performing and receiving the accolades that came with a good performance. I didn't know it at the time, and maybe because I felt like my practice time was forced upon me, but I was learning a very important lesson in accomplishing things I wanted in life. The lesson is called discipline. I had to put my practice time before my playtime. My mother would always say, "You can play after you've practiced your lessons". At the time, I thought her vigilance about my practicing was because she had bought a piano and paid for my lessons, and maybe even wanted to curtail some of the fun I was having with my friends. But, as it turned out, she was merely wanting to expose me to something she thought might be good for me to experience. And it was! As I said, I was learning how to set my priorities and discipline myself to routinely practice. I had to come to the understanding that I needn't put *minor* things over *major* things. (music students, no pun intended.) And as I matured, I was able to see the difference between the two, which is what childlike thinking cannot do. Because the childlike belief is based on, "if I rant and rave, or act defiantly, or become belligerent enough, I'll get my way". But my mama didn't play that. I wasn't going to complain, or be defiant, or act belligerently, and live to tell about it. So, my best option was to align my thinking with hers when it came time for me to practice my piano lessons. Life is that way too. You can rant and rave all you like, you can act defiantly, and you can be as belligerent as you think you can be, but Life doesn't let you get by without paying the price for your behavior. And sometimes the consequences can be life threatening. But if you put sound practices into your repertoire of behaviors you will find that life will not only honor your desires but will also give you a clearer vision of the outcomes from what you imagine is possible.

## Old Habits die Hard

Moving away from childlike thinking and behaviors requires practice in listening to that inner voice that guide you into mature thinking. That's not to say that all childlike thinking should be totally abandoned. Because your inner child is what keeps you mentally youthful, inquisitive, adventurous, and excited about life. And because children are so carefree, they tend not to perceive the gravity of what it means to act responsibly when it comes to making plans for their life. This is where proper guidance become necessary, in order to teach the childlike mind how to practice discipline. Because self-expression is so vital to your happiness, the more you practice self-discipline, the better you are able to understand yourselves and your capabilities. It's not a matter of if you will practice, it's a matter of what you will practice. Because you are either practicing "good" habits or "bad" ones. And I use the terms good and bad in reference to the maturation process. Good habits are the ones that serve you in the development of your true character and brings about self-awareness. Bad habits are the ones that chip away at your self-esteem because you've lost sight of who you are and your purpose in life. Good habits actually increase endorphins in your brain chemistry which give you the sense of well-being. Whereas bad habits can lead to addictive behavior disorders, depression, high anxiety, and psychosomatic disorders. Bad habits are generally developed based on a false perception of yourself, brought on by feelings of inadequacy, incompetence, self-loathing, or trying to please or impress others. Since all feeling are by-products of your thoughts, whether they are conscious or subconscious thoughts, mindfulness of your thoughts when you are tempted to act in an undisciplined manner could prove very helpful. Remember me saying I didn't enjoy practicing my piano lessons when I knew my friends were outside playing and having fun. Well, I could have sat there and felt "bad" the whole time during my lesson, or I could change my line of thought about what I was doing that would help me to not feel bad about it. Generally, when you feel "bad" emotionally, you want to do something that will stop that feeling. That is, unless you've developed the bad habit of wallowing in feeling bad. This is where it becomes important to examine your thoughts that are producing the feelings that you're experiencing regularly. In my case, the thought I held was about being in one place and wanting to be in another, based on the thought that the other place was better than the place where I was currently. And not until I changed my perspective could I move forward in feeling better about where I was and what I was doing. Oftentimes the ability to think through your current situation can be stifling when your feelings are very strong from thoughts that have been etched in your mind from habitual reinforcement. And it is only through discipline that will cause you to break from those bad habits and develop good ones.

## Insanity – Having Negative Thoughts and Expecting Positive Outcomes

Negative reinforcements are the thoughts and behaviors that support bad habits. They inhibit the ability to sublimate bad feelings into appropriate behaviors that negate the negative reinforcements. Because negative reinforcements survive on the autosuggestion of "I told you so's". It's done by taking a situation and twisting the data to fit the belief created by the thought of why you should feel bad. And each time you face a similar situation, it automatically starts the dialog in your head as to the expected outcome and your feelings about it. In these similar situations that nagging little inner voice of negativity starts its dialog with words something like, "here we go again". In order for you to break away from these negative reinforcements you must first come to realize that every situation is different. Of course, there may be similarities, but that does not constitute the current situation as being identical to a previous one. So, instead of jumping to a foregone conclusion, tell yourself that this is an entirely new situation and can have a different result than previous ones that seem similar. One thing that many people don't realize or acknowledge is that when they bring their preconceived ideas into a situation, it helps shape the outcome of that situation. You may have heard the concept of the self-fulfilling prophesy. Its basic tenet is that you create the result that you expect to find. The good news is that you can create the results that you want. But the bad news is that you can also create results not to your liking. And the reason why is because negative thinking gets ingrained into your thought patterns forming beliefs that are not conducive to using good judgment, making sound decisions, or incurring strong mental health habits. But, once you convince yourself that every situation is different, and approach it with open-mindedness, then you stand a good chance of seeing a different outcome and even having more options as to your behavior in that particular situation. Negative reinforcements have two enemies that you will do well to implore. They are commitment and persistence. When you are committed to seeing a difference, you will need persistence to keep your focus and not let anything get in the way of your desire before it's fulfilled. Persistence becomes your practice. I remember standing to the applause of the audience at the conclusion of my piano recitals and watching the proud expression on my mother's face. At that point, I got a glimpse of what it meant to not put minor things before major ones. And I knew that it was all the practicing I did that caused this event to happen and turnout the way it did. Because none of my friends who were outside playing while I was practicing got to experience what I did that evening. Not that they wanted to particularly, but I did.

Remember, you can also use autosuggestions to help remind you that each situation that you encounter is brand new. You do this prior to entering into any situation by saying something as simple as, "Life situations are life snowflakes, there are no two that are exactly the same.". The people may be the same, and the location may also be the same, but the energy that is brought to the situation does not and will not be the same. When I speak of energy, I'm referring to the attitude that one brings to a situation that is based on their expectations. Say for instance, you have a meeting scheduled to speak to your boss. At the last meeting you had with her, she chewed you out for not having done something she expected you to do. At this meeting, you can bring an attitude of "I hate this bitch", that will ensure fueling the flame of antagonism between the two of you. Or you can bring an attitude of, "I'm willing to cooperate with her", that may soften her criticisms, and help her realize that you are open to her recommendations on how to improve what you're doing on the job. Remember we talked about resonating with people. And we resonate with them on a vibrational level. So, if your objective is to create an environment where peace and tranquility is present, then you must bring an attitude that supports that end, or as the old saying goes, "you can catch more flies with honey, than you can with vinegar.".

## Let the Games Begin

While this session is on organized planning, and we have talked a lot about this process. I will advise you not to start thinking that this process is something else for you to do that has to be tedious. This process is as much about helping you to identify and stop doing whatever it is that you are doing that is blocking your path to a richer life. In other words, it will heighten your level of awareness about your "self" so that you can stop going through the motions of your daily routine living unconsciously and not getting what you want most out of life. All you're actually doing is *thinking* about what you want until it becomes a "burning" desire and maintaining a focus on what your imagination is revealing to you. Because what you focus on will prompt your behaviors. And that's all organized planning is, a set of behaviors that are designed to bring about the fulfillment of your desires with a plan that you yourself devise. You're the boss! Because your burning desire represents something you can't do without, and you won't rest until you get it. So, I invite you to relax and have fun with this process as though you were a kid with a brand-new toy. Keep in mind, that knowledge alone is worthless to you, unless it leads to the attainment of some desired outcome.

# DECISION – COMMITMENT TO FULFILLMENT

DECISIONS ARE LIKE a double-edged sword they can cut both ways. Good decisions are derived from analysis of the pros and cons of the effect it will have on you when the outcome is rendered. Poor decisions are just the opposite, there is usually no consideration given to the consequences of your behavior. Good decision may or may not be rational. But if they are considered irrational it's because it is aligned with a principle that you strongly believe in. All poor decisions are irrational because they are based on selfish motives and the gratification of some emotion that hasn't been dealt with effectively. Good decisions are like building blocks that builds self-confidence and a strong foundation for integrity. Poor decisions are like a wrecking ball in that they break down your moral fibers and instills carelessness, doubts, and self-justification. Good decisions foster self-respect and self-discipline. Poor decisions can lead to addictive behaviors and other mentally unstable conditions that depletes strong mental acuity.

The fact is, you are always at the fork of the road where a decision is required of you. Like right now, you are deciding to take the time to do some reading. Whereas you could have just as easily decided to have gone out for a five-mile run. And when you put this book down, you will need to make another decision about what to do with your time next. Now take into consideration that most of your decisions are based on preconceived ideas, which means that you've established some of your decisions based on previous experiences. These previous experiences can establish certain expectations. There's nothing wrong with that. Say for instance you decide to buy a pizza to have for dinner tonight because you know from previous experience that you and your family enjoy eating pizza every Friday evening. That decision is what some people might call a "no-brainer". It's a decision that is based on meeting your expectation, and the belief that it meets the expectations held by your family members. But sometimes people become too rigid in their expectations, and their decision-making is clouded by expectations that are no longer realistic and/or useful. The difference between realistic and unrealistic expectations is that unrealistic expectations are those you hold for yourself or someone else that you nor they are committed to. Such as, expecting your fourteen-year-old son to get all A's on his report card when he enters high school, while he thinks that getting C's are okay. His lack of commitment of getting straight A's comes from his lack of motivation. I had an uncle who attempted to use money as a motivator to get me to get A's on my report card. My mother put a stop to it because she wanted me to get good grades for some altruistic reason. In order to have realistic expectations of yourself and others, the commitment must be present and identifiable. And anytime you base your decisions on unrealistic expectations either for yourself or others, you are setting yourself up for disappointment.

I will now convey to you what Mr. Hill says are contributing factors in making poor decisions, and also the major causes of failure. Some are self-explanatory and require little elaboration. Many of them will be revisited so that you can see their full import. I want to point them out to you so that you can be aware of any ones you may be guilty of and need correction. Again, guilt does not imply condemnation, it simply means that you have identified something that does not serve your overall purpose.

1. Unfavorable hereditary background. Since you cannot do anything about what you inherited from your parents genetically, you may have to compensate through the assistance of others who you solicit as part of your support.

2. Lack of well-defined purpose in life. Your purpose in life is like your target. You need something to aim at.

3. Lack of ambition to aim above mediocrity. You will not have more until you believe you deserve more than what you're presently getting out of life. And you must be willing to pay the price for becoming financially solvent, or for having anything else worthwhile.

4. Insufficient education. True education is understanding how to organize knowledge into a plan that renders desirable results. Education is everywhere, but you must be willing to listen to its voice.

5. Lack of self-discipline. Immediate gratification is the greatest enemy to the development of self-control. However, if you want to implement a plan that gives you the opportunity to experience all the things you want out of life, you must be in it for the long haul; and thereby be willing to delay your immediate gratifications when it comes time to roll up your sleeves.

6. Ill Health. Taking care of your health implies that you believe in taking care of yourself, and conversely. Ill health doesn't necessarily imply that you are without any physical maladies, it means that you allow your maladies to control how you see yourself as having limitations.

7. Unfavorable environmental influences during childhood. "As the twig is bent, so shall the tree grow". Shaking free from early childhood influences that were not conducive to proper conduct may be quite challenging, but not impossible. That's why it may become necessary to surround yourself with people who know and appreciate what constitutes a healthy attitude toward living.

8.  Procrastination. Don't put off tomorrow what can be done today! One of the greatest obstacles to success is procrastination; because it takes away the momentum of working out an action plan that has potential benefits. It is also the biggest contributor to the illusion that there will always be enough time to get something done that needs to be done.

9.  Lack of persistence. Don't be like the people who get motived to start something, and at the first sign of defeat, they give up. I've said it before and I'll say it again, persistence is the *only* remedy for failure.

10. Negative personality. Many people develop negative personalities because they are dissatisfied with their lives and are always creating worst case scenarios in their heads and expecting them to happen. So, they become embittered and cynical about life and about people. Know that a smile is a frown turned upside-down. And also that in every nugget of defeat is a seed of success.

11. Lack of a well-defined power of decision. You can't go through life guessing and pretending to know things that you don't and become successful at anything you would hope to achieve. You must be knowledgeable and decisive about what's important enough for you to benefit from it!

12. Lack of controlled sexual urges. This may apply more to men than to women, but I'm not sure. I say this because men are visually stimulated more so than women. And living in an age where there is no shortage of sexualized images, it's understandable how a man can become distracted when stimulated by what he visualizes. Because what he sees that stimulate him, activates his imagination toward sex, and when the sex drive kicks in, it serves as a driving force that has the potential to distract him from taking care of business. The sexual urge is a powerful emotion that must be controlled through transmutation and converted into other forms of expression when the timing is inappropriate for engaging in sex. In other words, a

man must find his work gratifying enough so as to not succumb to his sexual urges during times when he needs to remain focused. Most artist, athlete, performers, and people in high positions of authority generally have high sex drives. That's because their position requires a lot of focused energy, and that type of energy is never far from their sex drive. But they channel that energy into their work ethic, and it helps them to maintain their focus on what they need to do to reach their goals. You show me a highly successful man, and I'll show you a man whose having lots of good sex during his leisure time.

13. Uncontrolled desire for "something for nothing." Some people have the mistaken idea that they can take shortcuts in life and thereby avoid doing things the "right" way, because it either takes too long, or it costs too much. Worst still, they may believe that playing by the rules is for suckers, and if you can get away with something, why not. There is no integrity or lasting joy in a person with this mindset.

14. One or more of the six basic fears. 1) Fear of Death 2) Fear of Failure 3) Fear of Intimacy 4) Fear of Being Alone 5) Fear of Getting Old 6) Fear of not having enough money to live on after retirement. The only cure for fear is faith. And the only faith that works is the faith that gives you the assurance that no matter what happens, Life's got you covered. But, don't have the conversation with Life that the baby had with his diaper. The diaper said to the baby, "Hey, don't worry I've you covered!" but the baby retorted back to the diaper and said, "You're full of shit."

15. Wrong selection of a mate in marriage. Let's face it, a lot of people get married for the wrong reasons. You may be one of them. And when two people are brought into a situation where intimacy is required in order for that situation to work, then personal as well as collective issues around intimacy needs to be worked out when they come to the realization

that the marriage isn't working as intended. Being married to the "wrong" person is about the worst relationship one can possibly put themselves in. Because you can be miserable all by yourself and not have to deal with the other person's anger and resentment. Marriage isn't for everyone. And staying in an unhappy, loveless marriage most always leads to a loss of ambition, motivation, and self-confidence. Poor relationships are the leading cause of addictions. Because people tend to overcompensate in other areas when they do not receive the love they desire.

16. Over-caution. This bears out the axiom, "Little ventured, little gained". Anytime you try something new there's always the possibility that you might not get it right the first time around. Also, there is some measure of risk in just about everything that you undertake. Even if it's walking one block to the mailbox and returning home without being hit by a passing vehicle driven by a motorist who just happened to be texting at the time. But, with the use of wisdom, you can take calculated risks when venturing into uncharted waters, that are far less risky than trying to "fly by the seat of your pants" type risks, which involves more guesswork than actual knowledge.

17. Wrong selection of associates in business. If you think of business leaders who galvanized the workplace into a place where employees felt they were a part of the organization, you have but to look at Bill Gates and his company, Microsoft; and Steve Jobs, and his company, Apple. Not only did they build two of the largest I.T. businesses in the world, but they revolutionize how people should be managed, via inspiration and self-motivation. If you are planning on going into business and will feel you need a business associate, then be sure to choose someone that you would want to work for. And select someone who complements the work that you do. So, if you are not proficient in some area, then select someone who is. If you aren't comfortable being out front promoting

your business, then select someone who has that ability. And above all, select people who believe in what you are about.

18. Superstition and prejudice. There is no rhyme or reason for why these two signs of ignorance still exist, besides fear. And there certainly is no place for them in commerce or when engaging with other people. You might as well believe in witches, ghosts, and goblins if you still believe in superstitions. Because the world operates on cause and effect, not on associating one thing that has no relevance to another. If I walked around the stadium complex where the Golden State Warriors play, and did it three times, that would not cause them to win, no matter how much I wanted to believe that it would. Superstition is much like wishful thinking in that way. And if by chance they do win, it was totally unrelated to anything I did. Some rituals may be symbolic, like wearing a Warriors cap, but it isn't causal. Prejudice is close-mindedness and will not help you get a clear picture of what's really going on when your mind is already made up.

19. Wrong selection of a vocation. Many people go to jobs that they do not enjoy simply because they receive a paycheck. However, no matter what the amount of that paycheck is, it is an extremely high price to pay for doing something during the majority of your waking hours that you do not enjoy. If you are one of them, you might want to think about planning your escape. The operative words being, think and planning. If you're not a thinking person, then stay where you are and collect your paycheck and pay the bills. But, if you dare to think about one day leaving, then start now and allow your mind to drift off into the realm of infinite possibilities. And if you are a young person who does not currently have a vocation, remember school advisors and even parents sometimes get it wrong as to what vocation you should choose. By all means select the one that makes you want to get up and go to class and learn about things that titillates your interest.

20. Lack of concentration of effort. There are many options to choose from in life. And that can create a problem for some people in that they can become immobilized by having so many options that they do no concentrate on becoming good at one. You don't have to holdout in order to hold your options open, because options are always open. But, in order to be successful, you must select from your options the one that you will place all of your concerted efforts into in order to take it to its highest level.

21. The habit of indiscriminate spending. People use money for all sort of reasons, some of which is to indulge their pleasures. This can create a problem when your pleasures become overindulgent and you're spending an exorbitant amount of money to maintain them. When you put your life plan into motion, it must take priority with everything that you possess, including your time and money. When you do so, it will validate the idiom, "Put your money where your mouth is", for you. Because to speak about your truth is to back it up with that which is of value to you.

22. Lack of enthusiasm. If you can't get excited about your growing success, then how can you expect others to believe in your dream. Life itself requires you to have a level of enthusiasm that will place your desires on the high priority list. The more enthusiasm you generate the faster you accomplish your goals. Because enthusiasm is like a blazing fire that looks to consume everything in its wake that would prevent it from achieving its purpose.

23. Intolerance. No one is required or should tolerate inappropriate behavior. But, neither should behavior that is different from our own be generalized to a populace as inappropriate. Diversity is the main premise on which life operates. Homogeneity exist out of cooperation and natural selection amongst cultural groupings, not from Life's attempt to make everyone the same. We live in a world where people can

cross borders from country to country and see how differently people live. But, at our core level we know that they are not much different from ourselves, because they also belong to the human race, which means they possess the same nature as ourselves. I believe that if you could remove the outer covering of every person, you would be able to see the same aspects of yourself in everybody.

24. Intemperance. Someone once said, "Too much of a good thing, is still too much of a good thing." Sometimes it's hard to know where the line is between enough and too much. Oftentimes the line is blurred by justification of thinking that you deserve more of one thing because you lack something else. Like the person whose love life is in the toilet, she may feel justified in having that second bowl of Ben and Jerry's ice cream because it compensates for something else that she's missing. Intemperance leads to unhealthy habits, and unhealthy habits comes from poor decisions. And the poorest decision one can make voluntarily is to not take control of their own life.

25. Inability to cooperate with others. When your ego goes out of control it affects your ability to work with and learn from others. You become stubborn and selfish in wanting to have things your way and your way only. This unhealthy attitude prevents you from seeing the value in others, whose value you may really need in order to meet your goals.

26. Possession of power that was not acquired through self-effort. This is basically speaking about power, or wealth that is inherited. This was clearly more obvious back in times when succession of power was handed down from a monarch to his heir. And in many respects, if the heir did not have good advisors that he listened to, he would end up doing more harm on the throne than good. Sometimes children inherit money from their parents or take over the family business. Those who tend to be successful in growing the business are the ones who

worked in it and started at one of the menial jobs. They came to know the business from the ground up by way of their early experiences. Many children who inherit money from their parents, if they were not taught the value of a dollar, usually wind up broke within a very short period of time.

27. Intentional dishonesty. Nothing ruins a person's reputation more than the loss of credibility. Dishonesty is a sign of insecurity at the highest level. It is the hallmark of someone who is incapable of trusting anyone, including himself. A dishonest person may get away with his shenanigans for a while, but there will come a time when his acts can no longer remain undetected. As the old saying goes, "The truth shall come to the light". Intentional dishonesty is also the leading cause of unhappiness because the dishonest person is filled with guilt and shame.

28. Egotism and vanity. As aforementioned, the ego wants its way. And it is often displayed through acts of vanity. There is a biblical verse found in Proverbs 16:18 that says, "Pride goes before a fall". When you begin to experience having the desires of your heart fulfilled, don't act in vane glory. Be humble and grateful for having a gracious entity, called Life (God), working in your best behalf to bring these things about. While you may have done your part in planting the seed, it is Life (God) that provided the increase.

29. Guessing instead of thinking. Guesswork will not help you succeed in attaining abundance. The attainment of wealth is not a haphazard undertaking. It is methodical and calculating, and you must have real answers to the questions that pertain to what it is that you will need to do in order to acquire the specific amount of money that you want. You gain these answers through the process of thinking. Your thoughts not only generate questions, but they also provide answers. And the more you think about something, the more focus your mind gets. And the more focus your mind gets, the greater

clarity you will have as to the development of your plan of action. Remember, the objective here is, *Think and Grow enRiched*, not guess and grow enriched.

30. Lack of capital. Every venture that you start where capital is involved, you will need a cash reserve, for two reasons. One, you must be able to cover the cost of your mistakes. And secondly, you want to be in a position to make purchases of products or services that are discounted well below market value that you stand to make a profit from. And perhaps there's an intrinsic value of having a cash reserve; because it may give you the feeling of success even before you've reached the level of success you intended.

Under this last one, you can list any particular cause of failure from which you have suffered that was not mentioned in the above list.

## I'll Get Around to It!

Of the aforementioned traits that get in the way of sound decision-making, the one I've dealt with most with my patients is procrastination. It's probably because it becomes so routinely easier to not do something different than what you are accustomed to doing. In other words, habitual behaviors get in the way of performing a new action. And some of these habitual behaviors can be elevated to addiction status. For instance, if you wanted to start eating a healthier diet, but can't do so because you are so use to the pleasures of an unhealthy diet. Knowledge alone does not help. Most people who practice unhealthy lifestyles, already know they do. A new action would require them to embrace the idea that a healthy diet can not only potentially prolong their life but can also help them to feel good physically. A lot of people do not change poor habits until they have experienced the agony of their poor decisions. Sometimes it comes to late. Some people think that if they don't make a decision it will grant them a grace period by prolonging the process of them having to deal with the issue before them. However, not choosing to decide is a decision to not make a decision. And procrastination gives one the illusion that they haven't made a decision yet. Procrastination also gives one the illusion that there is a time other than now. Not recognizing that now is the only time that there is. Yes, we make references to the past and future, but in actuality there is only the present moment. And the present moment is the only one you can experience. That is not to say that you don't ever change or evolve, it means that you evolve from the present. Or as the saying goes, "what you do today determines what happens tomorrow". It doesn't work in reverse order. You cannot do something tomorrow and be affected by it today. Nor can you do something today that will change what has happened previously. However, you can change your interpretation today of something that happened in the past. And this is especially useful when dealing with fear or anger associated with some past event. You can reframe your interpretation of the event to include factors that you hadn't previously considered. I mentioned in the introduction that while growing up my opinion of my father's parenting skills did not meet my standard for what I wanted in a dad. But today I have re-interpreted my experience because I now take into consideration that my father must have seen his role in the family as the provider, which he did adequately. So, that's where his energy went, and he left the emotional "stuff" for my mom to deal with. While he may have been emotionally unavailable, he did bring home the bacon. So, what does all of this have to do with procrastination, you ask? Well, it means that your focus has to be centered in living and making your life decisions in the ever-present now. It means that old ties to the past that immobilizes you from thinking about what is possible; and waiting for tomorrow to see if it's a better day for you to feel comfortable enough to make a change must be let go of.

## May I Borrow that Rabbit's Foot?

Another thing from the list of good decision-making inhibitors I will expound upon is the belief that you can have an impact on things that you don't understand, commonly known as superstition. I'm emphasizing this because many people were raised with the idea that there are certain behaviors which they can perform that will cause certain events to take place, or they can influence the outcome. I once sat next to a guy at a World Series baseball game. Toward the end of the game the home team was behind, so he turned his hat around and wore it backward, then he clasped his hands together and started to do what I assumed it to be, praying. I thought to myself, what if the fans who were rooting for the other team were praying for their team to win too. Which one would God listen to? And more importantly, who would God answer favorably, and why? And how could a fan with his hat on backward affect how the pitcher was pitching, or the batters were hitting? Because that's what determines the outcome of baseball games. But I bet you couldn't convince that fan that his hat had nothing to do with the outcome of the game. The bottom line is that it is an absurdity to think that illogical behaviors that are not directly related to an event can affect the outcome. It may seem trivial, but superstitions can be a powerful motive for acting in a way that give the person a false sense of persuasive power. I've never been to an astrologist, or a palm reader, or a Taro card reader. And I do know that every person has what you might call psychic energy, and some people develop that energy and become highly intuitive. And there are also a lot of charlatans who prey on the weak and simple-minded to cash-in on their superstitious nature. Reading your horoscope in Cosmo should not influence you to make a life-changing decision without careful consideration. Nor would it be prudent to follow the advice of someone whose only interest in you is self-serving. If you discover that you have adopted some superstitious behaviors, then act now to rid yourself of them. Use logic and reason if you have to, but at least ask yourself, "do I truly believe that what I'm doing will actually affect the outcome?" Then wait if you must for the answer to come from within. Because your spirit cannot support a faulty belief system with an answer that is untrue. Your spirit knows that nothing is fortuitous in and of itself, because everything is by design. For it to be otherwise would mean that there would be nothing you could depend on. It's not by chance that the sun stays at a certain distance to keep it from burning up the earth. It's not by chance that the air we breathe is a perfect mixture of elements that allows our lungs to take it in and release it. Life (God) orchestrates how things work in both the visible and invisible worlds. It's up to you and me to act prudently within the parameters of these governing laws of nature. And remember, if the rabbit's foot was all that lucky, then the rabbit wouldn't have lost it.

## Dearly Beloved, we are gathered here today to unite this man and this woman …

According to statistics, marriage by personal selection has a worse track record than arranged marriages. Whether you believe in arranged marriages or not, there is something to be said about having other people involved in the decision to get married. As aforementioned, people do get married for the wrong reasons. And it is these "wrong" reasons that are at the heart of every divorce. However, usually before the divorce occurs, there is collateral damage suffered on the part of both spouses. This damage can affect one's ability to think rationally and act in ways that support an unhealthy outlook on life. Or it can cause a general malaise feeling about what is truly desired. And it doesn't have to be that everything in the marriage is intolerable, in fact, most of the time it may seem to be okay. But, is okay really what you want? I remember counseling a couple and as I inquired about the state of their marriage, the husband, who was reluctant to come to counseling, blurted out, "for the most part, our marriage is not that bad". The wife jumped out of her chair and responded by saying, "And I don't want to be in a marriage that's not that bad!". In her mind that was the problem with the marriage in that her husband had settled for a lot less than what she wanted and expected. And she was willing to give up living with less than what she wanted if her husband was unwilling to reconcile their differences. She recognized that he had become complacent and together we identified it as his acceptance that things could not get any better in their relationship no matter what. In some marriages there are irreconcilable differences, and in some marriages things can be worked out if both partners are willing to look at their individual beliefs and the behaviors that support them. But there is no advantage to either party to stay in a loveless relationship, unless it's agreed upon that it is strictly a marriage of convenience. That way, the spouses are not living under any false pretenses that something exists between them that isn't really there. That way, both spouses can get on with their lives without feeling responsible or concerned for how the other person perceives their actions.

## Love Can Be Anything
## (Can't Nothing Be Love, But Love)

Love is the essence of our true nature. But love can take on many different expressions. It was the Greek philosophers who came up with three basic expressions of love. Philo, the type of love that may exist between a parent and a child. Eros, the type of erotic love that exists between a man and a woman. And agape, the type of love that transcends how people are physically connected, but rather how they are joined by the spirit. One might call agape love, divine love. And even though each type of love may have different forms of expressions, the foundation of all types of love is that the person expressing it cares for the person it is being expressed to. And that it is within our very nature to have the desire to express and receive love.

A few years back, my wife and I ended our thirty plus years of marriage. Not because we didn't love each other, but because we did. That may sound strange, but the fact that two people love each other doesn't guarantee that happiness will exist between them. Love and compatibility are generally what constitute the foundation for happiness to exist between two people, and when either one is missing then a mutual satisfaction will be forfeited. We realized that if we were to stay in the marriage, our ability to express the love we had for each other could possibly be compromised. It's when you come to the realization that if you and your spouse have maintained the friendship, but the marriage is not working satisfactorily, then it may be necessary to salvage the best part and let the other go. That's what we decided. Also, when you come to understand that the primary purpose of an intimate relationship is to help reveal aspects of yourself to you in the context of another person; because they are in a position of providing you with instant feedback regarding your actions based on their reactions to them. Which equates to two people supporting each other's personal growth in becoming the person they want to be. And, like everything else in life, things do change. Which means that sometimes your spouse can only take you so far on your life journey and after that you have to find other means of exploring the depths of who you are. There is an expression that addresses this dilemma, it says, "Some people come into your life for a reason, and others for a season." Which means that some people who come into your life may be there for only a moment and others may be there for your entire lifetime. My ex-wife and I will be in each other's life for the rest of our lives, just not as husband and wife. Because love is still at the foundation of our relationship even though we have found different ways of expressing our love to each other. You see, love has no interest in marriage licenses, or engagement rings, or even conjugal intimacy. Don't get me wrong, it's perfectly okay to have these things if and when the situation calls for them. But love's only concern is for the unification of all creation to be the perfect expression of its Creator in each of us.

## I Didn't Mean to do It!

Another thing that was mentioned as one of the factors for making poor decisions and failed experiences that I want to elaborate on is intentional dishonesty. Enough cannot be said about living with a lack of integrity. I believe it to be the most mental and spiritually debilitating of all the factors of making poor decisions and using poor judgment. If you haven't heard it before, you'll hear it now, "What goes around, comes around". Or, "Whatever a man sows, that he shall also reap." And there are other terminologies used to describe this phenomenon, like Karma, that's related to the issue of how you are affected by acts of dishonesty. Let me make this point perfectly clear, there is no way to enjoy the fruits of prosperity in the long run by means of dishonest gains. I didn't say that you could not attain wealth by being dishonest, you have but to look at the history of organized crime and see how millions of dollars were attained dishonestly. But most, if not all mobsters suffered tragic deaths, and not only them but members of their families also. Dishonesty is feed by the tyrant of selfishness that was created within the psyche when self-discipline went unchecked at an early age. When a child doesn't learn self-discipline and treat it as a moral value, then they presume they are entitled to have others cater to them and supply them with everything they want. So, they learn how to manipulate others in order to get what they want. And manipulative behavior can take on many different forms. The root of selfishness is the perception by the person that he is unloved and unlovable. So, in order to compensate for this lack of love, the person substitutes what they think they don't have for things they think they can get, by any means necessary. And there are exceptions. Some people can come from a loving family but may feel they were deprived of things they wanted as a child. So, when they get something, they are reluctant to share it, and they may even take something that doesn't belong to them and claim it as their own.

The leading crime in the U.S. is still theft. Not just the kind where someone robs another person's home, but also the kind where people steal from their employers. And some don't consider it stealing when they take things from their job. They think it's justifiable because they also think they should be earning more than what they are getting.

Or what about the more subtle ways of stealing, like when the store clerk makes a mistake and give you back more money than you are entitled to and you decide to keep it. Or what about when you do have a break-in and the thief steals items that you claim to your insurance were more valuable than they actually were. All of this may sound trivial, but the truth of the matter is that each time you act dishonestly, it erodes the part of your character that is responsible for building integrity. And integrity comes from the same root word as integer, which means wholeness. You can never be or feel like a whole person without integrity. You will be haunted by feelings of guilt, shame, and doubts when you lack integrity. That's why there are so many people with addictions, because they make every attempt to silence the voices of guilt, shame, and doubt. And the addictions are not just limited to drug and alcohol. They include every possible thing you can think of.

But what about unintentional dishonest? Intentional dishonesty is an act of planned volition, that carries with it the seed of deception. You might say that unintentional dishonesty is more about ignorance than deceit. Because if you don't realize that you're being dishonest, then you can't act with the intent to defraud. However, when it comes to life, ignorance of the laws that govern life does not give you a free pass when they are violated. So, what I'm saying is that if you are being dishonest and don't realize that what you're doing is dishonest, at some point this will be brought to your attention, either from within or from without. Life will not permit you to continue to act in ways that are detrimental to your well-being without pointing it out to you. It then becomes up to you to take heed and make the necessary corrections. As Shakespeare wrote, "To thine own self be true", we are reminded that if you can't be truthful to yourself, you cannot be truthful to others. And to be trustworthy is a most noble characteristic you can attain.

# PERSISTENCE – THE WILL TO OVERCOME ALL OBSTACLES

CAN YOU RECALL a time in your life when you were very attracted to someone and that person seemed to enter your thoughts all of the time? Even when you didn't necessarily want to think about them, you found yourself doing so. Well, that is the persistence of thought you need to achieve your goals in life. Your goals are so attractive to you that you think about them often. The other aspect of persistence that's needed to attain your goals is persistence of actions. When I was growing up, I found that the guys who got the pretty girls were not afraid of rejection, no matter how many times they heard the word NO. And the guys who couldn't get a date were the guys who were to fearful of rejection that they couldn't muster up enough courage to even ask. So, persistence of actions is like courting a girl, or guy, to go out with you. You must have a strong enough will that is connected to a strong desire in order to weather the storms of rejection. Life is a fair employer in giving you what you want, however you must prove that you want it bad enough sometimes. This proving that you want it is what separates the realists from the dreamers. The realist has a dream and awakens to put that dream into action. The dreamer has a dream and then goes back to sleep. It was mentioned before and I'll mention it again, that in order for you to get what you really want in life, you must feel as though you truly deserve it. Which brings me to another little story that happened to me.

## You Can't Always Get What You Want

When you think about why people miss-out on the things they want most, it has to come from the train of thought that they either feel as though they don't deserve to have what they want, or they believe they don't have the ability to obtain it. Now, these two thoughts do have sub-thoughts that support the major thought. For instance, if you feel like you don't deserve something, you may think it's because what you want isn't right for you, or that it's somehow bad for you. And if you believe you don't have what it takes to obtain what you want, you may back it up with the belief that what you want is reserved for the select few; or that you shouldn't pursue something "out there" because it may cause you to lose everything else you have in pursuit of it. Growing up I didn't carry the belief that I didn't deserve something that I wanted materially. I felt that most of the things I wanted were within my grasp, even if I had to wait a while to get it. But I did grow up thinking that there were certain girls that were out of my league. Status played a big part in this belief that I held. I remember one of my sister's friends, Gail Garrett, who I thought was the bee's knees, and I think most of the boys at Richmond High thought so too. Well, needless to say, she was a grade higher in school, and as I said a friend of my sister's which meant to me that she was off-limits to ask out on a date. There was no way I thought I had a chance to go out with Gail because I was just at the bottom of the totem pole being a freshman. But, the one consolation I got was that she was a friend of my sister and she came to our house occasionally. And yes, I would be there if I knew she was coming. So, basically my actions were controlled by my thought of what I did and didn't deserve. It had nothing to do with me being a nice guy who was beguiled by an attractive girl. That's not to say that my perceptions were totally unfounded because there was an unspoken pecking order that everyone understood and acted in accordance. But in order to get what you want most out of life, it oftentimes requires that you step away from the prevailing thoughts that support a system that dictate what people are expected to do and not to do within its boundaries, whether they are cultural or societal. I'm not speaking of the moral values that each culture establishes for the purpose of uniformity; but I'm speaking about the acculturated thinking that places certain limits on what a person can aspire to do and become.

Your primary objective in life presumably is to be happy. In order for you to be happy you must have self-confidence in your ability to achieve that which you want most out of life. And in order to achieve that which you want most out of life you must have a burning desire for it. Everyone is prone to be gratified in one way or another. And the fact is, you can be gratified in both your successes and failures. The difference is, with failure your gratification comes from satisfying your preconceived idea that whatever undertaking you engaged in that didn't work you can tell yourself, "I told you so!". But why would anyone want to gratify their excuses for failing, you ask? Because their excuses are the creations of their own imagination, and since they created them it feels to them only natural to justify them. There is a list of the most commonly used excuses that was compiled by a character analysis in the back of this book under **Appendix D**. I ask that you read them carefully and see if you use any of them as an alibi for failure. But with success, the gratification comes from knowing that you were persistent in your attempts to achieve your goal. When I was in the real estate business, I use to teach my associate the art of salesmanship. I would tell them that a client has to say "No" at least seven times before they gave up on a sale. For men it's like trying to date a woman who plays hard to get. He has to woo her and accept her rejections without giving in because he believes with all of his heart that her greatest admiration of him is his persistence. Or the woman who shows up every day at the place where she wants to be employed and inquire about the job-position she wants to fill believing with all of her heart that she is the best candidate for the job and that the employer will see her persistence as a virtue of how she gets things accomplished.

## You said You are Going to do WHAT?

Being persistent is nothing you haven't already done. However, if your acts to achieve something you want is not linked to a commitment to satisfy your burning desire to bring it into fruition, then you will persistently meet with failure. And some people who have become persistent at failing usually perceive themselves as victims of their circumstances. Failing to realize they are responsible for creating their circumstances. You won't be persistent at succeeding if you lack commitment. And commitment must show up and stand firm in those moments of your greatest challenges to give up. Because the connection between what you're doing is a direct reflection of who you perceive yourself to be. Some people have a fear of commitment. Why? Because true commitment requires taking a full measure of responsibility. It requires you to take charge of your life by controlling the temptations to practice bad habits; and exercising self-discipline to get the tasks done that need to be completed. When commitment is linked to persistence, they go hand-in-hand in carrying out your plan to attain what it is you want in life. These two are not only important in carrying out actions, they are also strong motivators in the maturation process as a whole, which involves maturing you into the next highest version of yourself. Every person is unique and has a particular calling. When I say calling, I'm not speaking of some agenda that Life has for you that you "must" carryout in order to satisfy Life. I'm speaking of a calling that stems from your very nature that seeks to freely express itself in your life by performing certain acts that only you can do. Remember, life is like gravity, it doesn't care if you jump out of an airplane with or without a parachute. But you might care. The same thing applies when it comes to choosing to listen to or not listen to your Spirit, or Intuition, or Inner-being, or whatever you want to call it when you receive Its message. You can choose to listen and heed the message or not. But, it comes from that part of you that gives meaning and purpose to your life because at that level of your being you know you are doing exactly what it is you came into this existence to do. And when you dismiss this calling you begin to make attempts to revert back to the illusions you had about yourself. And this starts the cycle of blaming your situation and circumstances in life on something or someone other than yourself. I'm reminded of the phrase the comedienne Flip Wilson used when doing one of his characterizations named Geraldine, when she did something that was deemed inappropriate, she would always say, "The devil made me do it!". As if this released her from being responsible for her actions. So, you too can blame the devil or anyone else as much as you want, but that won't change a thing for the improvement of your condition. Until you can see for yourself that you helped create the situations you find yourself in, then you will continue to impede your own maturation process.

## Thinking the Unthinkable

The idea of contemplation, meditation, or prayer may be a new concept to you. If so, that's good, because you may not have preconceived ideas about what it is or is not. If so, you may come to approach the idea a bit different after you've read this section. Some people think that meditation is making an attempt to empty your mind of all thoughts. However, my idea of meditation is to become an observer of your thoughts, without necessarily needing to know from whence they came or what they mean initially. Meditation is a passive activity with no goal intended other than allowing the deeps of your spirit to become more conscious to you. It is an observant process and not one of trying to control the direction of your thoughts. Some meditators accomplish this feat by having a focal point, which helps them to maintain a calmness that inhibits the mind from its incessant chatter of worldly matters. For example, you can focus on the point where your breath enters and exits your body. This is also a good way to become aware of being in the present moment. It is believed by some that meditation is the surefire way of reaching the inner most part of your being, because it represents a letting go of your human concocted reasoning. However, with contemplation, you can set an idea in your mind and try to look at it from as many angles as you can. This is where you can think of yourself as both the prosecuting attorney and the defense attorney in representing your ideas, and scrutinizing them as much as you like, and then becoming the jury to see what verdict you'll render. But not a verdict of guilt or innocence, but rather whether to pursue the idea further or not. Some people think of prayer as talking to God and asking for what they want; then it becomes a matter of waiting to see if they get it or not. A person once told me that God's answer to prayer requests can be either yes, no, or maybe. So, I asked him, then what's the point? If you believe prayer to be beseeching God to do something good that God would not ordinarily do, then you probably have a misconception of what *effective* prayer is. However, if you see prayer as a means of aligning your thoughts with Infinite Intelligence in order to express a desire that is a representation of your divine or true nature, then you're probably on the proper tract. I'm not speaking on this matter as a theologian, I'm simply using a term, called prayer, in an attempt to explain why you get the results that you do according to your belief system. Meditation, contemplation, and prayer all have one thing in common, they require you to block out thinking about the outside world and reflect on the thoughts, concepts, and ideas that are embedded in your subconscious mind about the nature of who you are. Your subconscious houses all of your beliefs and has a record of every experience you've ever had. But most importantly, it holds the blueprint of your true identity, or Divine nature. So, it's important to allow it to reveal to your conscious mind the significance of the particular thought, concept, or idea you are presently entertaining. I think you'll be surprised at what opens up for you when you do this. It may seem a little awkward or uncomfortable at first but stick with it until it isn't uncomfortable anymore. This is what it means to enter into the inner sanctum of your being. It is a practice that is designed to shut-out preconceived ideas and notions by mentally observing fresh ones that are far more effective in bringing fulfillment to your life. If your subconscious mind prompts you to do something, then get up and DO IT! Not only is timing everything, but your *commitment* to do your part is crucial.

Getting what you want out of life by mastering your thoughts and behaviors is not for the faint of heart. The faint of heart settles for as little as possible without high expectations for themselves. The faint of heart sits idly by and waits for something better to come along, knowing full well that nothing will. There is a verse found in Isaiah 40:31 of the Christian bible that say, "They that wait upon the Lord shall renew their strength, they shall mount up with wings as eagles; they shall run, and not be weary; and they shall walk, and not faint. Metaphorically, the Lord is the intuitive or subconscious mind that brings revelations to the conscious mind for those who sit in holy contemplation. Mounting up with wings as eagles refers to the conscious mind soaring to new heights once the revelation is received. Running and not growing weary means unbridled enthusiasm about the possibilities the revelation holds. And walking and not fainting means staying committed to the promise of the revelation's fulfillment by doing whatever is necessary to manifest it.

# POWER OF THE MASTER MIND – THE NECESSITY OF THE EMOTIONAL FORCES

MR. HILL DEFINES the Master Mind as: "Coordination of knowledge and effort, in a spirit of harmony, between two or more people, for the attainment of a definite purpose." His basic premise for this concept is derived from his observations of men who rose to financial prominence by associating themselves with others who, like themselves, were full of ambition. In today's fast-paced world, it may be a bit more difficult to find a group of people who might serve as associates in the development of your action plan. However, that is not to say that they are not out there, or that they have to be living in order for you to learn from them. And because of the internet and social media, you can reach far more people in a shorter period of time today than you could twenty-five years ago. Which means that you may not need a group of associates, but perhaps only one person who can offer helpful advice and monitor your progress. There is also a pool of retired businessmen and women who may be interested in serving you as a consultant or mentor. You can access books, podcasts, blogs, and YouTube videos on how to do just about anything. Granted you will need to tailor them to fit your particular plan, but they may be useful to help get you started. Remember I mentioned that knowledge alone is of no value unless it leads to a specific desired outcome. Well, this is what Mr. Hill is referring to when he says that knowledge must be used in a coordinated effort being intent on cooperation with those involved with you. This is where recognition and understand of certain personality types could prove beneficial. Because some types appear to be more difficult to work with than others. But, it's only because they are different from your own personality type. For some people decision-making is easy to do, for others they may find it quite difficult, particularly if they are fearful of making mistakes. So, if you don't find it difficult to make decisions, then you may find that working with someone who does to be helpful because they are more cautious and may see something that you have overlooked. And the same could be applied in reverse. Whether you choose to work with people whose personality is much like your own, or people whose personality is very different, the most important thing is that you are in agreement of the goals and objectives.

## Surfing the Net

Mr. Hill's concept of the Master Mind is also based on multiplying or maximizing your brain power. His approach was the formulation of a workgroup, because he surmised that six brains could produce more brain power than one. And he's right. However, today you don't have to know a lot about many things, you just have to know where to find it when you need it. The internet has revolutionized the availability of information. The search engines are so extensive with information that you can even find out information about yourself by googling you own name. Scary! However, with this proliferation of information, you can literally cut and paste together a document that you can use as your plan of action. You can subscribe to certain YouTube channels and get the latest information on a subject you may find of interest and useful for your action plan. You can even post an ad on social media asking for people to contact you who may have specific information that you need. As I said before, the people you want to talk to about what you're doing are people who have something to offer you by way of information that is useful. There are many naysayers out there who advice is designed to discourage you. Even those who think they are acting in your best interest by telling you that you shouldn't try something new. People speak from their experiences, and if their experiences have been based on fear, then their advice will be fear based. And there are charlatans out there who look to take advantage of you based on your lack of knowledge. So, be careful in selecting people you don't know in helping you to devise and work your plan of action. I would recommend that you use only people who can show you they have *proven* results in the area you're interested in pursuing. There are also books, like this one, that are helpful in encouraging you to step toward the perimeters of your comfort zone and discover a spectrum of possibilities. Take out a blank piece of paper. Now draw a circle, you don't need a protractor, it doesn't have to be perfect. In the middle of the circle place a dot. The inside of the circle represents your comfort zone, and the dot represents you located smackdab in the middle of it. The perimeter of the circle represents life. The perimeters are pliable and will either expand or collapse. Which one it does, depends on you. In order to expand the perimeters, you must be willing to move from the middle of your comfort zone out toward the edges. Because it is only when life feels you pushing on it to provide you with more, that it produces more for you. If you don't demand more out of life, then the perimeter atrophies, like muscles that aren't being used, and begin to constrict. So, when you're putting together your plan of action, know that you may experience some discomfort initially because you are stepping away from what's been comfortable to you for so long. But keep on pushing until the door of opportunity swing wide open for you to enter and bask in the joy of your new experiences.

## The Wise Traveler and the Unwise Traveler

As you think and grow enriched, you are in essence embarking upon a journey that requires knowledge, courage, faith, understanding, and cooperation. It's a great undertaking. And why shouldn't it be, because you are a great person. Become as the wise traveler who looks not only for the expected to occur on the journey, but is also prepares for the unexpected, and treats it as though it were a part of the journey when it happens. In an interview with World Heavyweight Boxing Champion Mohammad Ali, a reported asked him how he prepared for his fights. He said that he always prepared his mind to tell him to get up if he ever was knocked down. Because he understood that when you're down you have to have a plan of action in mind as to how you're going to respond before it happens. Preparing for the unexpected has made the difference between those who are successful from those who aren't. The unwise traveler who embarks on his journey is disturbed by the unexpected and seeks to blame the elements, or the terrain, or unfavorable conditions. This person adequately fits the description of a "victim of circumstances". The wise traveler sees the journey as wanderlust, filled with everything needed not only to survive, but to flourish. The unwise traveler sees the journey as drudgery, filled with angst, and lacking the essential needed to be content. The wise traveler sees challenges along the way as a means to gain new insights and strength from them. The unwise traveler sees challenges as a means of validating his insecurities and therefore complains about the misery he perceives himself experiencing. The wise traveler knows that he is never alone on his journey and envisions all objects as a sign of Infinite Intelligence guiding and directing his path. The unwise traveler often feels alone and lonely because she thinks she is a separate entity from the Source of All that Is, and that she must struggle along without acknowledging or expecting Divine interventions. She sees the objects on her path as elements that are working against her. The wise traveler exercises courage when it comes to expanding her comfort zone beyond its borders. She knows that in order to expand her horizons there will be times when she will feel uncomfortable and vulnerable, but she's not bothered or interrupted by it. She is willing to risk the disapproval of others in favor of following her heart toward her charted destination. The unwise traveler holds on to his fears and remains stuck in a place that feels familiar, even at the expense of being unsatisfying. When he does creep along, it's often at the insistence of others whose approval he seeks; only to land him in a place that is equally as unfulfilling as the place from whence he came. The wise traveler is undaunted by seeing the road coming to an end because he knows that when he can no longer walk it, he will take wings and fly. The unwise traveler is not only afraid of her road coming to an end, but she is mortified as to how it will end. And her life is consumed with how to die rather than how to live. The end of the journey is home. The wise traveler goes home in peace because she has made peace with everything along her journey. Being at home is the culmination of having brought love, truth, peace, beauty, and gratitude into the world. And even though you may not be able to give the world all the love it needs, the world needs you to give all the love that you have.

## The True Source of Knowledge

Mr. Hill states that when knowledge is coordinated in the spirit of harmony toward the achievement of a specific objective, then the parties involved "place themselves in a position through that alliance to absorb power directly from the great universal storehouse of Infinite Intelligence". This statement by Hill coincides with a biblical teaching found in Matthew 18:19 when Jesus says to his disciples, "That if two of you shall agree on earth as touching anything that they shall ask, it shall be done for them of my Father which is in heaven.". Which conveys that the power of Infinite Intelligence can be accessed whenever the spirt of harmony is invoked among people. I believe harmony to be the highest form of pleasure our soul can experience on an individual level as well. Because when our mind and body are in full cooperation with the soul's desire to express itself, which is our divine nature, then the experience we feel is truly heavenly. And the only reason this experience is not continuous is because the ego is allowed to convince you that it can do better. The ego is the spokesperson for the false image of yourself that it created. It created this false image from the thoughts and ideas of people around you and extrapolated from these ideas what would make you appear to be not only acceptable to these people, but also creates the illusion that it makes you appear to be something other than who you are. Part of this process of morphing into an image acceptable to the people around you is based on the desire to have an identification with a particular culture, organization, or society that promote thoughts, beliefs, and ideas that appear reasonable to you. But the other side of that coin that gets people to conform is based on a deep-seated fear of being ostracized. All people have a need for belonging, some greater than others. So, the thought of being excluded plays a big role in their decisions to act in certain ways. Like motivation, conformity in and of itself is not a problem. Conformity is needed as a means to formulate cooperation among people, otherwise there would be disorganization that leads to chaos. However, when conformity cause one to lose their personal identity, then problems ensues. Because your personal identity is intertwined with your personal beliefs and values based on your interpretations of your experiences and the conclusions you came to about them.

## Your Attitude determines your Altitude

How high up on the ladder of success you climb is up to you. More importantly, what you define as success and how you measure it is necessary if you are to carry out a plan of action to acquire things that you desire most. Suppose you defined success as becoming a millionaire. Did you know that if you earned $25,000 a year and worked for 40 years that you would end up becoming a millionaire? However, it would require you to save every dollar that you earned during those forty years, which in all probability you wouldn't. However, it is one option. My point is that by definition you decide what success is. And your attitude will determine if you succeed at being successful. And what exactly constitute your attitude? It's the feeling you have toward something you're involved with based on your thought about it. If you are enthusiastic about doing something, then you might say that you have a high attitude, or a willing attitude. If on the other hand you approach something with trepidation, then you could say that you have a low or reserved attitude. And keep in mind that others can usually read your attitude. And some people even feed off of your attitude particularly if you work in close proximity to them. So, the clearer your definition of success is to you, the better strategy you will develop to attain it. And the better the strategy, the more enthusiasm. And the more enthusiastic you are about your plan of action, the more cooperation you will get from others. Enthusiasm attracts people to want to be a part of something they consider to be worthwhile. And enthusiasm can spread like wildfire within a group of people who believe in what they are doing. The plan you develop may start with you, but in order to garner the support of others you will need to get them on-board with your idea. Some people that you get involved will go along just for the ride, until the ride gets too bumpy and then they may bail. But, with your demonstrated enthusiasm and your inclusion of benefits that they will derive from being a part of your plan of action you can generally get people to stay devoted to completion.

## A little exercise in Role Modeling

Here are some basic questions that may help you to gain clarity of your definition of success.

1.  Who do I know that I believe is living a successful life?
2.  What do I admire most about this person?
3.  What do I perceive about their approach to life in general?
4.  What do I perceive to be their most valuable attribute?
5.  How do I think they might react under pressure?

6. How would I describe their intelligence level?
7. How do I perceive other people responding to them?
8. What seems to be the driving force in their life?
9. If I could only ask them one question, what would it be?
10. How long do I think it took this person to get where they are?

If this person is not someone you know personally, you probably can do a little research about them. And if you don't have anyone in particular in mind, then pick someone from something you have an interest in and find out as much about them as you can. Not the gossip about them, but about their rise to success. If the person is someone you have access to, then ask them if you can conduct an interview with them. Write down a list of questions that you would like to ask them that will help you see what's involved in moving forward with your plan of action. Take a proactive approach in associating yourself with success.

I'm not a big football fan, but I do respect athletes who plays the game with dignity, and one such player in my opinion is Drew Brees, one of the National Football Leagues all-time greatest quarterbacks. Brees was given an award by the Sports Writer's Association for his prowess on the football field. However, Brees showed why he is not only a great football player in his acceptance speech, but also why he's a great human being. He said that the things he tried to practice every day and also teach his three sons were Gratitude, Humility, and Respect. What a contrast to the teaching of entitlement, competition, and conquest as some children are taught. So, it's no wonder why he is a great football player, because he is a great man who practices the things that lead to greatness. People sometimes think that one has to accomplish great feats in a particular activity in order to be considered great. However, greatness is not measured by what one does on the outside, but rather who one is on the inside. And in order to develop a character that can be characterized as great, one must actively practice the things that will make it happen. When a doctor opens his business to the public, it is said that he now has a medical practice. The same for a lawyer, he practices law. And even though they are involved in very different pursuits, they are both practicing in their respective professions. And depending on how they practice, which means their integrity and work ethic, will determine the quality of their services. The same is true for the practice of gratitude, humility, and respect. They must be practiced until they become second nature to you. Which in fact is part of your true nature. I remember growing up and how my parents taught me to say, "may I", "thank you", and "please". And to the adults it was "yes mam" and "yes sir". And to this day I find myself saying these words because gratitude, humility, and respect were also a part of my practices growing up, even if I didn't realize at the time the value it held for me later in life.

# THE MYSTERY OF SEXUAL TRANSMUTATION – PROFITING FROM THE USE OF SEXUAL ENERGY

MR. HILL'S BASIC description of the phenomenon of sexual trans-mutation is harnessing and directing sexual energy into actions that will accomplish a specific desired outcome. This concept may ap-pear new to many men, but women have been doing it for ages. Why? Because the women who were blessed to have a high sexual libido were not held in high esteem, particularly in western cul-tures, so many of them found creative ways to gratify their sexual desires. These women generally exercised one of three basic op-tions. They either did not care what people thought about them and their sexual mores. Women like Margaretha Geertruida MacLeod, better known as Mata Hari, who used her sexuality as an exotic dancer and courtesan. She was later executed in France, not for prostitution but for being accused as a German spy. Other highly sexed women who wanted to avoid the shame of societal miscon-duct went underground. There are tales of slave master's wives slip-ping out at night and having sex with the slave men. These men certainly could not divulge they were involved in such activity be-cause the penalty for their action would cost them their lives. Some women had their sexual trysts with men who could not kiss and tell because they themselves were in a committed relationship. Or these women would choose a so-called respectable man in a position of authority who might jeopardize his position if the word got out. I wonder if this is the premise of what happened in the biblical story about the woman who was caught in adultery. In order for her to have been caught, meant that she must have been with the man at the time. But only she was brought forth to be stoned for her "crime". Perhaps the man was a high ranking official in the church and ordered that she be stoned as a means of keeping the truth from surfacing by burying it with her. Her so-called crime goes back to an ancient Mosaic law that basically implies that if adultery is committed between a man and a woman, it is because the woman seduced the man. And of course, he wouldn't be able resist her. And this particular Mosaic law was based on a story written by the same man Moses in the book of Genesis. It says that the first woman on planet Earth, Eve, tempted her gullible husband Adam, to eat the forbidden fruit, which was taken from the tree of the knowledge of good and evil. If we interpret this as an allegory, we can better understand something about human nature. Adam represents the thinking part of man while Eve represents the receptive feeling part. The tree represents man's freedom of choice. The forbidden fruit represents the sexual appetite of man. Sin represents ignorance. Technically, sin means missing the mark. And the way you miss the mark is by being pointed in the wrong direction. And the world represents man's consciousness. Therefore, man's sexual appetite is first aroused as a *feeling*, and then he *thinks* about how to act upon it, based on his choices. If his choices include blaming someone else for his actions, then he truly has missed the mark. The same applies when sex is misused, it is always based on man's lack of understanding. So, sin enters man's consciousness through a lack of understanding that is acted upon, which produces guilt and shame.

It's not falling into deep water that drowns a man, it's staying submerged in it. The same is true of ignorance. It's not the realization that you are ignorant in certain matters, it's choosing to stay submerged in it that produces guilt and shame.

## I'll Take Door Number 3 Wayne

The third option for the women who enjoyed the pleasures of sex but couldn't handle the scandal or was unwilling to risk being caught in an adulterous tryst used transformation. They sublimated their sexual energy into something else they wanted to achieve. Some women became stalwarts in many organizations in their communities contributing to a number of lifestyle improvements, some became entrepreneurial and started businesses that earned them a high level of respect in their respective areas. And some became warriors for causes they believed in fighting for. While these means show how women transmuted their sexual desires in a positive way, those who did not see these types of opportunities transmuted their sexual energy in ways that lead many of them to the next best thing, food. Even today, many women experience weight gain from their diet because they use food as a means of substitution for sexual gratification. Food was a natural alternative because it satisfies in many ways. It offers a variety of flavors, textures, and colors. And when one is satiated, there comes a feeling of contentment. And a really highly sexed woman enjoys cooking because she gets to play with all of the ingredients. It's like foreplay to her. But, seriously, the transmutation of sexual energy is something that can produce fantastic results of something you want to achieve because the finished product feels almost orgasmic. Now you understand why I can hardly wait for this book to be completed.

## Whatsoever Wild Oats a Man Sows, that Shall He also Reap

Mr. Hill pointed out that most men who attained their fortunes did so after the ripe old age of forty. He states that it is during this period in a man's life that he better comprehends how to use his sexual energy, even if he came to understand it by accident. While I agree with Mr. Hill that age can be an important factor in bringing about a change in one's perception of sexuality, I also think that the environmental climate about sex has been another important factor that has influenced many men's decision on transmuting their sexual energy. The sexual revolution of the mid 1960's helped influence a number of people to look at sex in a much healthier way. Not only was sexuality experimented on in the streets, but also in the laboratories. There were sex studies conducted and human sexuality classes taught on college and university campuses. The adult film industry began to flourish because people became less inhibited to explore their sexual fantasies. Adult bookstores began popping up across the country, where you could purchase all manner of sex toys and sexual aids. Wife-swapping and Swing Clubs and parties became a means some people used to spice up their love life. Things like chatrooms became open forums for people to talk about sex and for getting together to have sex. Men don't have to suffer from erectile dysfunctions because of the proliferation of male enhancement drugs. And there's also hormonal medications for women. And sexual image can be found almost everywhere, books, magazines, billboards, you name it. But most importantly, sex became more easily accessible to the average man. From licensed boudoirs to massage parlors that offered the happy ending, men were able to sow their wild oats without having to spend an inordinate amount of time searching for a sexual encounter. Also, the growing number of women who were entering the workforce didn't perceive sex as strictly being limited to marriage as did many of their predecessors. The Women's Liberation Movement liberated the thinking of many women about demanding equality in the workplace; and it also liberated many women's thinking about their role in the bedroom. It's as if a switch came on and made it acceptable for women to initiate a sexual encounter. But even with sex becoming more acceptable as a means of self-expression, doesn't mean there is no longer a need to transmute the sexual energy. Because, as was mentioned earlier, whenever sex is misused it is because of man's ignorance. Also, because the sexual urge is still the highest form of stimulation mans' brain receives, it makes him highly susceptible to sexual obsession and addiction if it is not brought under his control.

## Sexual Healing

Looking back at the sexual revolution of the '60 it's important to note what the revolutionaries were up against and how you view sexuality in light of those past events. Also, to recognize that not all of the seemingly archaic sexual values of the baby boomer's predecessors were unwarranted. Some of the drilling against pre-marital sex came from concerned parents who were afraid of their sons and/ or daughters having an unwanted pregnancy. Some concerns were centered around contracting a venereal disease. HIV and AIDS were not around back then, but syphilis and gonorrhea were the two major threats from having unprotected sex. Most of the baby-boomer's parents didn't understand much about sexuality and considered sex a topic that was not to be discussed openly because it was considered very private, and to some even taboo to talk about. And God forbid that a woman be labeled promiscuous, because her reputation as a "respectable" woman would automatically be ruined. Most of these values about premarital sex came from puritanical beliefs that sexual activity was a corruption of human decency because it appealed to the sinful nature of man. (The sinful nature was supposedly the part of man that always chose to do that which God, as defined by the religious communities, deemed as inappropriate behavior.) And, it was believed that the potential for a person becoming sexual promiscuous adversely affected their self-perception as well as giving them a misperception of their partners. This belief was primarily directed toward women and became known as the double-standard between men and women's sexuality. It is now argued that these beliefs were engendered by males as a means of controlling female sexuality. In other words, men didn't want a lot of loose women running around having sex whenever they wanted to. That was supposed to be left to the discretion of the man as to when a woman was to have sex.

Many men already felt that it was distracting enough for them just by having sexual desires for a woman, let alone knowing that there were woman out there engaging in sexual activity whenever they wanted. How distracting would that be? Not only was pre-marital sex an issue that was hard for men to deal with; but judging from some of the old TV programs from the '50 and early '60 that prohibited networks from even showing a married couple in the same bed, you'd think that post-marital sex was an issue as well. So, the question that behavioral scientist asked was, how did the attempts at controlling human sexuality affect people's sexual behaviors? The answer was revealed by the on-set of the sexual revolution. The false pretenses that vilified man's sexual urges came under attack.

## What's Love Got to Do with It?

Sex is just sex! It is an activity that is engaged in and enjoyed by both married and unmarried people. And for those without a sexual partner, autoerotism is a viable option. Also, when sex is coupled with spirituality it becomes sexuality. Which means that the sex act is taken to a higher or deeper level of pleasure. And what happens when romantic love is mingled in? Mr. Hill had this to say, "Where love, romance and the proper understanding of the emotion and function of sex abide, there is no disharmony between married people.". In other words, disharmony occurs when sex is misused for egotistical purposes. But when it is used as a means of expressing sexuality at the spiritual level, then both parties are united in a way that brings harmony to the relationship. This is the area where a woman can exert most of her influence with her partner, and it will either make him or break him. This is not to say that a woman should try and control a man with sex. It is to say that the woman is the receptive half of the sexual equation, and as such, her sexual responses to a man sexual needs will play an important part as to whether he feels appreciated by her. If a woman uses her influence as a means of support on a frequent basis, she can literally help create a genius. If she uses her influence harshly and negatively, she can help create a monster. In other words, a woman who chooses to remain sexually inhibited or ignorant of the male sexual response will eventually cause him to lose sexual interest in her. She might as well pass out her husband's cellphone number at the single women's retreat on how to get a man. Men are hardwired to please a woman. Whether he goes golfing and comes home and boasts to her about his low score, or whether he brings home flowers, he does so because he wants her to be proud of him. If she refuses to understand that men are wired to please a woman, then she will treat sex as her wifely obligation and not as a means of keeping him desirous of her by letting him know in his innermost being that he is the *man* in her life. The only men who will tolerate being miserable in a loveless, sexless, non-romantic marriage, are the men who are deathly afraid of being alone. And in all probability think that this is the only woman who will ever have him. While love is experienced in both the mind and emotions, it still may not be enough to bring mutual satisfaction and contentment into a marriage, and neither will sex alone. You can love someone and not be in love with them. Being in love means that you want to share all of yourself with them and they with you. And since we are sexual beings, then this includes that aspect of ourselves as well. It is the combination of love and sex that quenches the soul's thirst for complete union between two people. Mr. Hill states it this way, "When these two beautiful emotions are blended, marriage may bring about a state of mind closest to the spiritual that one may ever know on this earthly plane.". Mix in a healthy dose of romance, and it is inconceivable of what a man is capable of accomplishing when he is utterly satisfied in this manner. Awesome!

## Love and Happiness

Love and romance are introduced because they both are significant ingredients in the transmutation of sexual energy. Without them, when the sexual desire becomes activated, one may find themselves looking for love in all the wrong places. Therefore, the sexual energy isn't transmuted, it becomes the driving force to behaviors designed to satisfy the physical aspect of sex only. There is nothing inherently wrong with a man satisfying his sexual desire, however as the sexual tension builds, other things that are of importance will get put on hold until the sexual desire is fulfilled in one way or another. That's why the necessity of love is important because transmuting sexual energy isn't easily accomplished without a real strong motivation. Even the promise of love may be enough to motivate a man to make achievements that he believes will attract women. Mr. Hill examined things that stimulate the mind and motivate behavior. He listed the top ten as being those that are most freely responded to, they are:

1. The desire for sexual expression.
2. Love.
3. A burning desire for fame, power, or financial gain, money.
4. Music.
5. Friendship between either those of the same sex, or those of the opposite sex.
6. A Master Mind alliance based upon the harmony of two or more people who ally themselves for spiritual or temporal advancement.
7. Mutual suffering, such as that experienced by people who are persecuted.
8. Autosuggestion.
9. Fear.
10. Narcotics and alcohol.

The top eight of these ten stimuli are natural and can be construed as constructive, and the last two are unnatural and destructive. In Mr. Hill's analysis, he states that the desire for sexual expression is not only the top stimuli, but he states that it moves a man to action more than all of the other nine combined. The analysis has validity because it is backed by three strong possibilities that accounts for the sexual motivation in men.

1.  The propagation of the species
2.  Health benefits, both mentally and physically
3.  Transformation from mediocrity to vibrant living

The innate desire for man to procreate is the foundation of mans' sex drive. If sex was not extremely pleasurable, there would be little desire to engage in it often if something else felt better. The health benefits are unparalleled. The activity of sex produces more endorphins in the brain than any other activity known to man. These endorphins can reach a very high level in a youthful man and make him feel almost invincible. Also, the physical body can reap the benefits of sexual activity through movement and tension release. It's impossible to feel both pleasure and pain at the same time. Judith Sachs says in her book, *The Healing Power of Sex,* that sex can be life-affirming. From her studies on the subject, she reports that, "Life-affirming sex with a compassionate partner is good for you. It can take the place of medicine, and its effects can be long lasting. It can quell such demons as loneliness, anxiety, tension, timidity, depression, touch deprivation, psychological trauma, and alienation. It can actually relieve chronic pain, stiffness, body ache, and insomnia and alleviate certain skin disorders. It can restore you to yourself." With so many benefits sex has to offer, we should be setting up sex clinics all over the country. Transformation is achieved through transmutation of the sexual energy into other energy sources that are used to accomplish a certain task. It basically takes the focus off of the performance of a sexual act, without diminishing the energy that comes from being aroused, and placing that energy into something more productive. Show me a man who has made outstanding achievements in his life, and I'll show you a man who has learned the art of sexual transmutation.

# Spirit in the Dark

While sex has the ability to give a person immense physical plea-sure, it can also be a highly spiritual experience as was mentioned earlier. This spiritual aspect of sex is what constitutes the mystery of transmutation. It involves the spirit, mind, and body in an interplay of energy movement and vibrations. It is inconceivable to think that you can transmute your sexual energy into another form of energy to be used for any other purpose without your spirits' involvement. Because your spirit is responsible for supplying all of the energy that's available to you to be used for whatever purpose your conscious mind dictates. It is the part of you that never sleeps nor slumbers. It is your lifeforce, your energy producer, and your reality creator. Think of your spirit as analogous to the hard drive in your computer. Every aspect of your computer is dependent on the hard drive. It pro-cesses all of the data, organizes it, and interprets it in a way that the mind comprehends what the data means. Unlike your hard drive, your spirit's operations are unknown to the human mind. It operates in total secrecy. But the images it impresses on the mind give some indication that there is a definite connection between the world of the visible and the invisible. You might go so far as to say that your spirit is the most personal impersonal part of you. What that means is your spirit represent your true nature and all of the expressions that goes along with that nature, which makes it very personal. However, your spirit is not concerned with the things the mind ordinarily concerns itself with, at least not in the same manner, which makes it very im-personal. For instance, if your mind concocts some hair-brain scheme to get rich quick, you probably are concerned about how you'll ben-efit from your actions, and you might also be concerned about the consequences. But the spirit isn't concerned with benefits and con-sequences, but rather the motivation of your actions. Because if your motive isn't consistent with your true nature, then your spirits goes to work in trying to bring it to your consciousness. However, it is your mind that distinguishes and chooses which voice it will listen to. And there are only two voices. Your spirit's voice and your ego's voice. So, when it comes to the expression of your sexuality or anything else under the heading of self-expressions, your spirit will always provide you with a motive that is consistent with your true nature, and the expressions will always feel very natural. The ego on the other hand will provide you with a motive that's selfish, self-centered, and need I say it, egotistical. Don't get me wrong, your ego per se is not your enemy. But, neither should it be treated as your master. When it is under control your ego can actually be a dutiful servant in the assimilation of information that could very well serve a noble purpose. But when it is out of control it can portray your personality as something that resembles the characteristics of a robot rather than a human being, in that it lacks the quality to empathize with others. So, if you have a big ego, you better also have a big stick to keep it tamed.

## I Dream of Jeannie

Sexual attraction comes from within and is reflect by others who match that mental imprint. And when two people's mind imprints match, then we have what is called chemistry. And literally when a match is made, the chemicals in the brain activate your sexual response. That doesn't mean that two people who are attracted to each other immediately want to jump in the sack. It means that they become more aware of their mental and physical states due to the aroused desire from connecting with a source that matches their internal image. It's like a woman who stands mesmerized in front of a storefront window gazing at a beautiful red dress. Not only is she attracted by the dress, but perhaps as much by the color of the dress, if red happens to be her favorite color. Or a man who stares in admiration of a little black sportscar because he likes the color black, and also sportscars as will. My point is that everyone has preferences that are unique to them. And their attraction is made possible by the imprint embedded in their mind of what they like. There is no rhyme or reason as to why someone favors the color blue over the color grey. There may be an association that can be traced back to childhood where one remembers their first encounter with a blue toy that they liked. But that is not causality for liking the color blue. They still may have liked the toy whether it was blue or not. But because it was blue it may have made a more lasting impression on their mind. The same can be said for people that you find sexually attractive. Having said that, I'll say this, all people are sexually attractive in one way or another. Some people have attractive eyes, some hands, some feet, some hair, and so forth. These attractive features may not stay the same always. People get older and facial and bodily features change. But as you know, beauty is in the eye of the beholder. When I was younger and whenever I saw what I considered to be a pretty woman who was head over heels in love with a man who was not distinguishably handsome, I'd say to myself, "I wonder what she sees in him?". Little did I know at the time, that what she saw in him was not visible to the naked eye. And even though physical appearance change, to the couple who have drank from the eternal fountain of each other's love, outward appearances become less important to them. Because they will have cultivated the spiritual connection between themselves and formed a deeper bond. And with this deep relationship comes the capability to transmute sexual energy.

## Let's Give Them Something to Talk About

Of all the issues that therapists get from their patients, the one that produces more guilt and shame is based on sexuality in general and pre-marital sex more specifically. Not so much with the younger generations, but mostly with the baby boomers who were drilled with the notion that sex before marriage was immoral and therefore prohibited. And it's not that they didn't have pre-marital sex, it's that they still carry the guilt and shame for having done so. The guilt that their parents and a puritanical society inflicted on them. And the shame of not being able to openly talk about it to the very people who considered it as a wrong thing to do. This sexual prohibition mostly applied to females however males were also shamed for being with the "wrong" kind of girl. It's ironic that this same generation of people who were inundated with guilt producing sexual ideas became the founders of the sexual revolution in the United States. And let's not forget religions contribution to the prohibition of sex before marriage. Or it's prescribed method of having sex. Meaning there were sexual behaviors that even a married couple shouldn't perform even with each other's consent according to canon law. Some people were led to believe that God not only disapproved of pre-marital sex but was even offended by those who practiced it. This is not an indictment against religion in its attempt to keep people from misusing sex. However, many religions seem to have taken the sex act to the extreme by making it appear to be an unnatural act if it is not done in the prescribed way the religion says. But these prohibitions didn't stop, or even slow things down from people having sex before marriage, it just pushed it underground making it a secretive thing to do. And when something is kept in secret it can't be openly discussed. And since it could not be openly talked about, it increased the guilt and shame for not only having done it but denying it when confronted in order to avoid judgment and scorn. Some try to assuage their guilt by going to confession and making a claim to have had sex. They are prescribed a penance for their deed, and no one is the wiser except the priest, so it seems. This may ease the immediate guilt, but it won't erase it. Because their guilt is internalized and doing something external won't eliminate it, especially if they don't plan to stop having pre-marital sex. It is not in the best interest of mankind to ascribe sex as the villain for man's moral decent. Ignorance is the culprit, not sex. Sex is the most beautiful activity two people can engage in, whether they are married or not. The sexual chemistry between two people does not require a marriage certificate. However, marriage may represent to the parties involved, a long-term commitment, if that is what they both want.

So, in order to transmute sexual energy, one must be willing to re-evaluate their thoughts about sex in order to let go of the guilt and shame associated with it. If you had sex prior marriage, which most people have, or if you are having sex and you are not married, then ask yourself, would you have felt any differently toward the person you had sex with if you were married to them? If your answer is no, then chalk it up to having brought pleasure to yourself and another because it was not intended to do harm, if it was a pleasurable experience. If it was not a pleasurable experience, then chalk it up to your inexperience to distinguish between being with someone who you didn't have chemistry with versus someone who you might have chemistry with. If your answer is yes, that you would feel differently toward your sex partner if you were married to them, then look at the experience as a marriage of your spirits with your partner's that culminated in a pleasurable physical act. In the realm of the spirit, no marriage license is required, only mutual consent.

## You Show Me Yours and I'll Show You Mine!

You learned things about your sexuality at a very young age whether you were aware of it as sexuality or not. From the time you first touched yourself "down there", you formed an opinion about what that feeling was like. And because it's a high pleasure-zone, you more than likely enjoyed touching yourself. Perhaps you spoke with your parents about what you experienced, or maybe a sibling or a friend. During my era, most parents not only didn't bring up the subject of sex, but they seemed to avoid it altogether. So, many of us had to find out about our sexuality the best way we could, without much parental input. I recall being astonished the day I stumbled across my dads' Playboy magazine. I didn't learn much about sexual intercourse, but I did learn about the prelude to it. Which for me was becoming aroused at looking at those beautiful nude bodies. Many people of my generation carried around the guilt and shame surrounding their sexual behavior because they were led to believe that they should not engage in it casually. Even though it may have felt very natural, it was deemed inappropriate, at least until you were married. It makes you wonder about the number of people who entered marriage strictly to get a license to have sex and thereby circumvent the guilt and shame allegedly associated with having "casual" sex. Or those who thought having a marriage certificate would rid them of their current guilt and shame from their pre-marital sexual exploits? That's like using marriage as a form of penance that would absolve you of previous "wrongdoings". If the divorce rate in the U.S. is any indication of the people who got married in order to "legitimize" sex, then I would make a conservative guess that at least 50% of all marriage were entered into for this reason. Because, sex alone cannot hold together a troubled marriage. But, let me just say, that if sex was the reason you did get married, then don't feel guilty about it. Recognize it for what it is and go from there in developing a sound relationship if that's what you want. It probably wouldn't hurt to get professional  help for you and your partner in order to identify and resolve other issues that may have been a part of your decision to get married. There are people who get married for reasons that are just as irrational than wanting to have sex. Like, getting married for status purposes, or to have someone to control and order around. At least the sexual act is natural. And even though sex cannot shore up a shaky marriage when there are other issues that need to be addressed, having a spouse who enjoys having sex with you as much as you do with them can create a strong incentive to build a strong marriage if at all possible.

## Hang up your Hang Ups

The reason for bringing this subject up about pre-marital sex is to make you aware that if you still harbor thoughts of sex as being dirty, immoral, sinful, or anything like that, then you still carry the guilt and shame associated with sexuality. Which means that the energy you are using in your sexual practices is tainted with guilt and shame, which are the enemies of a healthy attitude toward sex. And you do not want to transmute this kind of negative energy into your plan of action that supposedly will bring more satisfaction into your life. It cannot happen. Because your level of enjoyment would be greatly diminished by your guilt and shame even if you somehow managed to acquire great wealth according to a plan you devised. Because guilt keeps you focused on past behaviors with the shame of regret. You must first purify your thoughts about sexuality by consciously accepting that no matter what previous sexual acts you performed, you did so with a person of consenting age and maturity to know what they were consenting to. That way you would have met the condition of not having taken advantage of another by using them in a demeaning way. However, if this was not the case, and you knowingly took advantage of someone sexually, then you must exercise forgiveness for yourself and the other person(s) involved. Forgiveness is the only means of purification for prior actions that were not representative of your true nature. Forgiveness does not mean that you necessarily must forget your prior actions, nor abdicate taking responsibility for them, it means that you've come to realize that your offenses against others and against yourself are not acceptable to you because they did not represent your true nature. Forgiveness will not necessarily relieve you of the consequences of your behavior, but the consequences of guilt and shame will not apply. Forgiveness does provide you with the means to not be emotionally devastated by whatever consequences you face.

# THE SUBCONSCIOUS MIND – THE KEY COMPONENT OF REALITY

IN BOTH PHILOSOPHICAL and scientific terminology the unconscious mind is often interchanged with the word or concept of the psyche. The word psychology derives its name from this word which literally means soul. So, psychology is the study of the soul. This study is done from both a systematic cognitive and behavioral approach. The terms mind, body and spirit are generically used to refer to the total composition of a human being. Psychoanalysis, a theoretical construct on understanding human behavior postulated by Sigmund Freud, refers to this triad as id, ego, and superego. The superego would be the unconscious mind that maintains moral values and tempers the actions of wayward desires. In New Thought ideology the unconscious mind is the residence of Infinite Intelligence that defines mankind both individuality and collectively as being an expression of Itself. While this concept still acknowledgements man's freewill, it assumes that the unconscious mind (spirit) provides insights and guidance to man in the direction of expressing his true nature, while fostering and nurturing the connectedness of all humanity. Whereas Mr. Hill makes the distinction between the unconscious mind and the subconscious mind which he describes the subconscious mind as the field of consciousness that gathers data from the five senses and classifies, records, and stores the data for use by the conscious mind. He further states that the subconscious mind acts on impulses and impression that the conscious mind sends it by way of desire. And the subconscious acts on the dominant desires that are mixed with feeling. Which means that your emotions come into play as to whether you want something bad enough in order for your subconscious to take you seriously and manifest that desire into its physical equivalent. So, in Mr. Hill's analogy the subconscious mind is not just for storing data, it is a data processor. Most importantly, Mr. Hill exclaims that, "you cannot entirely control your subconscious mind, but you can voluntarily hand over to it any plan, desire, or purpose which you wish transformed into concrete form.". That statement should be music to your ears. Because it gives you the opportunity to chart your course for leading a life that is self-fulfilling. As the New Thought Ideology implies, the subconscious mind interprets its data into a language the unconscious understands and acts upon it by way of Infinite Intelligence. This Infinite Intelligence lodged in the unconscious is the power that transforms the invisible energy of thoughts into the visible physical world, and It knows no limits or boundaries.

## Thanks for the Memories

I want to point out here that the subconscious mind is indivisible, but there appears to be three major operational components that the subconscious employs. One component is what controls your autonomic nervous system. Which is the system that controls your internal functions. This means that you do not have to consciously think about making your heartbeat, or your lungs to breathe in air. Another component your subconscious uses is the part that relates to memory and preprogramming. Every experience you've ever had is logged into your subconscious with a label attached. That label represents the conclusions you reached about every experience you've ever had. It's kind of like a tab on a folder in a file cabinet. So, if you have another experience similar to that of a previous one, you can automatically review your findings and develop your current plan of action. In other words, you rely on this part of your subconscious to provide you with the information you placed there so you don't have to reinvent the wheel. The effects of the experiences are what creates the memories. And you can preprogram your subconscious mind to allow you to remember something that you held an intense focus on. So, if you saw your grandmother make a peach cobbler, and you wanted to learn how to do it yourself, you paid strict attention to what she was doing in the preparation. This paying strict attention is how your preprogramming is done. The third component used by your subconscious is the one I refer to most. This is the part of you that follows the blueprint of your true nature. It is the part that is constantly making attempts to raise your level of awareness of who you are and what your purpose in life is. If the biblical statement, "The Kingdom of Heaven is within you" resonates with you at all, then this is where you will find that kingdom, in your subconscious mind. This aspect of your subconscious never sleeps nor slumbers and cannot participate in anything that is not divinely ordained, your conscious ego mind can, but it can't. Which simply means that every situation that the subconscious creates for you is in perfect alignment with the natural order of things. It is indeed the Most Holy Place that you will ever know, because it is the direct linkage to the unconscious mind of Infinite Intelligence. Your subconscious can be thought of as both your servant and your master. As your servant it materializes your every desire that you have preprogrammed into it according to what you have accepted as your reality. And as your master it never waivers from sending you messages about the truth of who you are by way of situations it creates for you and mental impressions that are designed to pique your interest; all prompted by the Infinite Intelligence of the unconscious mind. So, the next time you find yourself in a situation that seems a bit uncomfortable, instead of asking "why is this happening to (2) me", do the math and double it, by asking "why is this happening for (4) me". What is it that your subconscious wants to reveal to your conscious mind that will help you to see yourself in a more positive light?

## To Tell the Truth

There was a popular TV game show back in the '50 called *To Tell the Truth*. It was based on a panel of four people asking a series of questions to three contestants in an attempt to correctly guess the true identity of the person the contestants claimed to be. And of course, only one of the contestants was that named person. So, I thought it would be befitting that we approach this subject during this session on the subconscious to see how it helps to influence you toward detecting truth that will set you free while avoiding the consequences of poor choices. One of the age-old questions that still hovers over mankind today is, "What Is Truth?". That illusive thing that seems to defy a pure definition that is satisfactory to everyone. The problem most people have with this thing known as truth, is that what's true today may not be so true tomorrow. Especially when it comes to human behavior. That's the basis for my profession is that people do change. Even though your basic personality remains pretty much intact, the ability to change your behaviors stem from changing your thoughts about who you see yourselves as in relationship to your environment. It's just a matter of whether you are making changes consciously or unconsciously. And I'm using the word unconsciously to mean that you behave in a certain way without giving it much, if any, thought. Because we live in a changing universe, everything must change, adapt, and adjust accordingly in order to survive. Needless to say, those who don't adapt very well, if at all, don't survive very long. It's a part of what nature provides in all of creation. For instance, you can take a brown rabbit from a desert environment and place it in a snowy environment, after a generation or so, those brown rabbit's fur will turn white like the snow. This is because the rabbit adapts to its environment, and the white fur provides the animal with protection from being easily detected by predators, as well as provide an insulation for maintaining heat.

Truth is somewhat like beauty, but rather than being in the eye of the beholder, it's in the mind of the beholder. And what you distinguish as truth is directly related to your consciousness called awareness. In other words, you cannot establish truth on something you're unaware of, unless that truth is that you know you are unaware of it. The mere fact that you acknowledge something establishes it as a truth for you. Whether you like the thing or not, or whether you believe in it or not, it doesn't matter, it's a truth as long as you acknowledge its existence. Even when an atheist says he doesn't believe in the existence of god; the fact is, he has already established the existence of something he claims not to exist. Perhaps what he means is that he doesn't believe in the concept of a god that was presented to him by someone who made an unconvincing presentation. Holding on to truth is like trying to hold the wind in the palms of your hands. You can feel it as it moves, but you can't hold it in one spot, because it's everywhere and nowhere at the same time. Sometimes the wind moves gingerly and at other times as a mighty force. The effects of truth are similar. Sometimes it's ever so gentle and you ponder over it sometimes for minutes, hours, or days; and other times it stirs you to act right away. It has been said that life can change in the twinkling of an eye. But that type of change occurs when you are confronted with a life changing truth that disrupts your routine of business as usual. Such as with what's happening now with the coronavirus pandemic. It is causing everyone to rethink what they are doing, and what they should do.

## Do You Promise to Tell the Truth, the Whole Truth, and Nothing but the Truth?

In Neale Donald Walsh's epic book, *Conversations with God*, it chronicles a dialogue he has with God. In one of their discussions God reveals to Walsh that there are two types of truth, absolute truth and relative truth. This absolute truth is without rival or equal or opposite. It is what it is and is unchangeable. In other words, it is what constitutes the law that governs everything in both the seen and unseen realms. However, the effects of this absolute truth may be experienced differently from person to person, but the law that govern it is eternally the same. This absolute truth can be expressed and understood as the activity of Infinite Intelligence, that which created and sustains all of creation and everything that supports it. Relative truth on the other hand is subject to affects only in the physical domain. Relative truth is what gives you the opportunity to apply meaning to the experiences you have in life. Because nothing as it pertains to relative truth has any meaning except the meaning you gives it. So, with relative truth comes choices. You can either feel hot, cold, or warm. You can go up, down, or be somewhere in the middle. But, with these choices, you can't be two at the same time, and that's what defines your experience in that moment of what you think is happening. It pertains to your emotions as well. Remember you can't experience pleasure and pain in the same moment. And just because you cannot experience two emotions at exactly the same time, does not mean that the opposite of what you're feeling is irrelevant. When relative truth is examined from a so-called moral psychological perspective, some people attempt to treat it as though it were absolute truth. They get into an either/or mindset. Such as, thinking something is either right or it's wrong; it's good or it's bad; it's holy or it's evil. And to those who use this line of reasoning it may be useful for them, but it's still relative truth and does not apply to everyone. Only absolute truth applies to everyone. You may know of the polar opposites, but usually people develop a preference of one over the other. For instance, some people like hot weather and some prefer cold. And there are a myriad of temperatures to enjoy in-between the two extremes. Some theorist espouse that it is absolute truth that holds the two opposites of relative truth together or makes them one and the same thing. It's like the warm temperature is what holds hot and cold together, or in-between holds left and right together. If indeed Absolute Truth is the activity of Infinite Intelligence, then they would be one and the same. However, the absolute truth offers no judgment one way or another. A crude example of this could be a natural disaster where many lives are lost. Does that mean the natural disaster was wrong, bad, or unholy? It could be described as unfortunate for those who lost loved ones. And perhaps even tragic for those living in the aftermath of such devastation. But, to ascribe it with a moral inscription is ludicrous. There was even talk when the AIDS epidemic began that it was a curse sent by God to get rid of those who engaged in homosexual activity. How asinine was that idea? And what about this coronavirus, does it have moral implications? Whereas I do believe that it does have significance in shaping our moral values, but the virus itself isn't moralistic. And what about people who pathologically lie, cheat, or steal, is there a life-threatening disease for them too? Not necessarily, but there are consequences for such behaviors. But, when it comes to Absolute Truth, it is not based on human opinions, speculations, or definitions. It is the measuring stick that man has to stand up to in order to come to terms with who and what he truly is. And it is your subconscious mind that is directly linked to absolute truth. There is no other way that you can come to know it!

## Please, Give Me a Moment to Think about That

This phenomena of attempting to understand absolute truth from a relative truth perspective is indeed a mystery. Because the process of how mysteries are brought to light goes beyond human reasoning. There is a biblical text that refers to this mystical phenomenon that says, "spiritual matters are spiritually discerned." Which means that you can't figure out the workings of the spirit with mentally devised constructs no matter how logical they may seem to you. Your subconscious mind knows and understands that it is part of the mysteries of life, and therefore does not need to rely on human intellect to render them useful. This spiritual component of man is capable of turning man's intellect into his servant and not allow it to become his master. As Rudyard Kipling states in his epic poem, *If*, that speaks about the contrast between relative truth and absolute truth, he says, "If you can dream - and not make dreams your master; If you can think - and not make thoughts your aim; If you can meet with Triumph and Disaster; and treat those two imposters just the same." He is speaking about how the intellect can be disillusioned by the relative truth of its own creation and treating them as though they were absolute truth. But when the intellect becomes your servant, then you'll know what it means to make allowances for life's mysteries and to revere them as the source of power that they are. When you plant a seed in the ground, it is not the seed nor the soil that provides the increase; but rather a power that is unleashed within the seed that causes it to explode in order to receive the rich nutrients from the soil, the water, and the sun. The same explosive power that is in the seed is also in the sun, moon, stars, and in you. Mechanics say that a gas engine is started by a controlled explosion when gas is ignited by a spark in the combustion chamber. You too are able to think, move and be alive because of a spark that's ignited in you that may be referred to as the Breath of Life. Because when the Breath of Life leaves your body permanently, you will have performed your last physical activity.

## I Don't Know What to Believe Anymore

To believe in the invisible realm of life may be difficult to grasp, especially if you haven't contemplated the relationship between mass and energy. And to have faith in its operation may be even more challenging to your current mental state; particularly if you hold the idea that "seeing is believing". The difficulty lies in the simple fact that the invisible realm is shrouded in mystery and is undetected by the senses. You may sometimes find yourself acting on the assumption that if you can't detect something with your five senses, then it must not exist. But perhaps you can get a glimpse of the invisible realm with your soul's eye by way of comparison to things that you are familiar with in the physical domain. Perhaps then you will become more susceptible of making the leap to believe in the invisible realm of life itself and why everything in the physical realm is derived from it. If you have any electrical devices, you operate them because the invisible thing called electricity supplies them with the power they need. If you have components that operate using Wi-Fi, then you know there is something invisible that allows for the connection to be made from one device to another. So, similar to your Wi-Fi connections is your subconscious mind to the realm of the invisible. It takes your thoughts and translate them in a way that produces matter. Accepting that this process exists is absolutely necessary, not how the subconscious does it, but that it does is what's relevant. Because your conscious mind will not submit to anything that it doesn't understand. Also be ever mindful that your subconscious mind holds the blueprint of your true nature, and it is always active in producing situations for you to help reveal this nature to you consciously. It will also respond to your impulses. That's why autosuggestions and affirmations are beneficial practices. Because it literally gives the subconscious mind something to chew on that you placed there deliberately. When you place a thought into your subconscious mind and do not experience results right away, don't think that nothing is happening, because it is. You may benefit from going over the session on faith again if doubts and/ or fears arise. When you experience problems, you want them to re-solve quickly. However, sometimes what you see as a problem may actually be something you need to experience in order to see some-thing about yourself that you wouldn't be able to see if this condition didn't exist.

# THE BRAIN – THE RECEIVER AND TRANSMITTER OF THOUGHTS

OUR BRAIN WORKS in conjunction with our creative imagination and our subconscious' power to manifest our thoughts into physical forms. Our session on thought revealed that we live in a pool of thoughts, just like a fish that lives in water. They surround each of us, and they are vibrational in nature. And it is virtually impossible not to be affected by them. Just like you are incapable of being unaffected from the sound of a gunshot. The vibration of the shot rings in your ears, and you are more than likely to have a thought as to what that sound means. In other words, thoughts are like radio signals that are transmitted from a radio tower to your radio by means of vibrations in the air, thus we call them airwaves. The only way you can hear sounds is by vibrations that stimulate the inner ear. The brain operates in very much the same way. The thought vibrations are received by means of sensors in the brain that respond to a certain vibrational pitch. The higher the pitch, the more receptivity in the brain's receptors respond. The thing that controls the level of the pitch are emotions, both positive and negative and everything in-between. Have you ever noticed how you become much more alert when you are around someone who is exhibiting the emotion of intense anger? Or how you become a little bit more self-conscious when you are around someone who shows you great admiration? Your brain's response is based on the vibrational signals it is receiving from the other person's thoughts. Mr. Hill speaks about mental telepathy and clairvoyance as a natural means of communicating the intangible.

## I Heard It Through the Grapevine

The brain detects a thought and either accepts it as relevant or rejects it as irrelevant. If it is accepted, the brain then transmits the thought to the creative imagination and a plan of action is constructed. Once the plan of action is drawn up it is transmitted to the subconscious mind where it is supplied with the necessary ingredients and the power to manifest the plan into its physical equivalent. If this all sounds highly technical, well that's because it is. The way the brain detects thoughts is through nerve cells located in the cerebral cortex. It is estimated that there are between 10,000,000,000 and 14,000,000,000 of these nerve cells, all arranged in a definite pattern. With such a highly constructed communication system in the brain, it is inconceivable to think that it was devised to only be used to attend to the daily functions of the physical body. This is why science continues to delve into examining the higher capabilities of the human brain and its elaborate communication system. More on this will be discussed in our next session on The Sixth Sense. But for now, simply try and grasp the concept that your brain is receptive to the thoughts that come from another's brain.

The creative imagination part of your brain devises its plan from the vibrations transmitted to it by your thoughts and feelings. And most importantly, it is the feeling aspect that intensifies the thought vibrations. Remember we said that your thoughts alone will not produce that which you want most. It has to be coupled with a burning desire. This burning desire is the feeling that in essence raises the vibration of thought and tells the creative imagination that you are determined to have it manifest. The most effective way to turn your wants into a burning desire is by knowing consciously that you deserve to have what you want. The Rollin' Stones message in one of their hits songs is, "You can't always get what you want". By-in-large there may be some truth to that, however, without question you always get what you *think* you deserve. So, stop thinking that you deserve less than what you want. I'm not promoting a sense of entitlement here that says the world and everyone in it owes you something. Because they don't! I'm speaking of having a sense of self-awareness that brings into play the things that you desire as being self-expressions of your true nature. So, if you desire a big house because you naturally like to entertain, or you need a lot of space to move around in, so be it. The creative imagination is influenced by the thoughts that are free from doubt. This is why the practice of autosuggestion and affirmations are useful. Because they help negate negative thoughts that you hold about yourself and your ability to have what you desire most. Your creative imagination is no respecter of person, it will act on whatever constitutes your belief system.

## "If I only had a brain"

The subconscious mind, though it works in conjunction with your brain, it is not a part of your brain functioning. It supplies your brain with the things it needs to do its work, but it is not subjected or affected by anything that the brain does or does not do. Then how does the subconscious mind work in conjunction with the brain if it is not a function of the brain, you ask? Let's look at a character from a familiar children's story called The Wizard of Oz. The character we'll look at is the scarecrow, who was devoid of having a brain. So, he joined with Dorothy and the others to find the all-powerful wizard of Oz to obtain a brain from him so that he would be able to think. But, when he arrived at Oz and spoke to the wizard, he discovered that his actions along the way indicated that he really didn't need a brain. The message here is that when you are acting in ways that depict your true nature then your brain's functions are put on autopilot. Your brain constitutes what you are aware of, but your subconscious mind determines what you become aware of. Even though your subconscious is you, it is not controlled completely by the "human" aspect of your being. It knows no boundaries or limitations, and it never waivers from the divine laws that govern life. Your subconscious mind is that invisible substance that lives and move and has its being in you. Make no mistake about it, your subconscious always has your human best interest as its mission, but it will not override the will of the conscious mind until it absolutely has to. The foundation of its operation is love. The kind of love that defies definition, because it is all inclusive. Someone once told me that white is not the absence of color, but that it includes every color. Love is like that. It includes the expressions of every person, place, and thing, even when it appears not to be present.

## Let's Get into the Habit of Breaking Bad Habits

You brain establishes neurological pathways that transmit both chemicals and electrical currents through the brain by way of synaptic gaps. These gaps are the areas between neurons that hold substances emitted when one neuron fires, sort of like a gun going off, until it is absorbed by another object, a process called reuptake. And this process continues, in milliseconds, along a pathway until it reaches the end and evokes a physical or mental response. This means that certain events triggered by thought, whether conscious or unconscious, causes these neurons to fire. For instance, if you witness a car accident where someone is injured, your thought could prompt you to take immediate action where you call for help, or your initial thought may lead you to have an emotional response due to the injuries you see. These responses are the result of your brain activity that know what your response will be based on stored information, or a response that is conveyed from the autonomic nervous system. This system automatically kicks-in when the threat of danger is present. Its basic two responses are fight or flight. If there is a perception that the eminent danger can be dealt with by fighting, then the body will stand poised for battle. But if the perception of the danger is that it's best to leave the scene, then the body will supply the necessary adrenalin to get you out of there. But we are looking at these neurological pathways to see how they are used in establishing the patterns of behaviors that you've developed, and for those that you would like to develop.

Your brain function doesn't distinguish between fact and fiction. It treats everything as if it's real. Whenever you have an emotional response from some fantasy you entertain, it's because your brain processes it as the real deal. That's not to say that you consciously can't distinguish fact from fiction, it's only to say that your brain treats all thoughts in the same way. So, basically, during the times you are engaged in fantasy, it feels a bit like reality, until you tell your brain to stop processing the fantasy and you come back down to earth. That's why dreams seem so real, because the brain is projecting images that your mind perceives as actual events. Well, all of your past experiences are now a part of your history. They do not exist anymore, except in your mind. And you can treat past memories as fantasy or as a nightmare, it's completely up to you. My point is that you are responsible for what goes into your brain for processing. You choose what concept and ideas to accept and which ones to reject. Granted, some ideas and concepts are so compelling that it's difficult to distinguish their validity and/or value; but with the guidance from your subconscious mind, at some point something about the idea or concept will feel natural or it won't. And when it doesn't feel natural you must be willing to table it even if you have placed a physical or emotional investment in it. To do less would mean that you develop a bad habit that will at some point prove its unproductive toward obtaining what you really want. Alcoholics don't start out as an alcoholic when they take their first drink. They may have a predisposition for alcoholism if it has a genetic link. But the average person who becomes an alcohol developed the habit of drinking because they are unwilling to change their behavior because the disease of alcoholism clouds their judgment. And somewhere in the deep recesses of their mind they accepted that it was alright to be an alcoholic even if they won't admit to it openly. It may have gotten established as being alright to be an alcoholic because that may have appeared to be the lesser of the two evils. Rather than becoming someone else they were afraid of becoming, which to them was worse than being an alcoholic. At least as a drunk they had a built-in excuse for behaving badly. It's kind of like the Dr. Jekyll and Mr. Hyde character. Just like Dr. Jekyll, when the alcoholic drinks his potion he becomes someone else, even if he doesn't remember who he was the next morning.

## I Like It like That!

Until we accumulate some years under our belt, most of our life experiences are based on trial and error. If you try doing something and it seems to work, you may be more inclined to seek situations that are similar in nature and try it again. Conversely, if you try something and it does not seem to work, you may scrap it and file it away in your memory bank as unworthy of your time. In either event, similar situations you find yourself in will trigger either a positive or a negative response depending on how you perceive the outcome will be. Now let's suppose that you are wanting to accomplish something that you've never done before. This may be the very reason you bought this book. Your brain has not yet established any neurological pathways because you have not yet attempted to make any interpretations of what it is that you're doing. So, let's begin by establishing what you want to do as being very meaningful to you. You are clear about what it is that you want to accomplish, and you are starting to feel that burning desire we talked about. Since your brain treats every thought as though it were rooted in reality, then the object of controlling your initial thoughts are crucial in terms of the pattern you want your brain to establish based on how you think and feel about what you want and how badly you want it. You want those neurons to fire in the direction of rendering a positive result each time you are involved with your plan of action.

## Try It, You Might Like It!

Getting back to trial and error, if you try something that you had in your plan and it doesn't render you the results you expected, realize that knowing what doesn't work is a valuable piece of information. You don't want the brain to establish a pathway down the road to failure, by thinking that something works when in fact it doesn't. I like what Neale Donald Walsh had to say in his book, *Conversations with God*, about handling resistance in the mind. He said that if you want abundance and you affirm it in the now, but your mind rejects it, then affirm that your abundance is on its way. This way, it negates the mind's argument of not having abundance now, because it cannot disprove that abundance is on its way. I said earlier that you mind will not accept something that it doesn't understand, and that's because the pathways have already been long established. So, you must make it palatable to your mind to keep it from going down that pathway and drawing conclusions that aren't helpful. And again, that's why clarity of your desires is so important because if you don't have something you want because you previously didn't know how to get it, your pathway to not getting it has already been established. Therefore, you have to establish new pathways and allow the old ones to become suspended and eventually atrophy. This is also where autosuggestions and affirmations play an important role in helping your brain to establish pathways that are triggered by thoughts that you consciously placed in your mind. Remember nothing in this realm of relativity has any meaning except the meaning you give it.

## F.E.A.R. – False Evidence Appearing Real

The greatest detriment to not listening to your subconscious mind is when fear has a strangle hold on where you allow your thoughts to go. When things aren't going well in life, some people are tempted to start thinking of the worst-case scenarios. And it's perfectly okay to do that. If you can handle the thought without freaking out. And the sole reason that will keep you from entering the valley of "Now I'm screwed", is that you find motivation in proving that voice in your head and other people who doubt your ability, that they are wrong. So, in other words, fear can serve as a motivator, but PLEASE do NOT try to use it as a teacher. The lessons that fear teaches are hazardous to your health and must be avoided at all cost. There was a lady who came to see me who was going through a divorce. She said that it took her by surprise when her husband asked her for the divorce. During our session she reported that it shouldn't have come as a surprise to her because she always feared that one day he would leave. She just didn't know when that day would come. I told her that the divorce was not totally her fault even though she held that fear. And I also told her that because of her fear she could not recognize what she was doing that may have been a contributing factor in her husband's departure. That's how fear works, it blinds you from seeing your potential and the potential of others. It insidiously creeps into the mind and robs you of your joy and sense of well-being. Because fear can operate so subtly, some people go through their entire life not recognizing they are shackled with fear. Because at some point having fears became normal to them. Some people think that the opposite of love is hate. But actually, love's opposite is fear. Hate is a subsidiary of fear, but hate doesn't inculcate all of fear's expressions. The expressions of love sets' the spirit free, and fear's expressions imprisons the soul. Mr. Hill lists six fears that he believed were the worst ones. He refers to them as the Six Ghosts of Fear. I will list them for you and give you their symptoms so that you can exam yourself and see if you possess any of them.

## Public Enemy #1 – Fear of Poverty

Whereas poverty and abundance are on the same plain as all opposites are, however, they point in completely opposite directions as all opposites do. My point is, you cannot move toward riches while thinking about being impoverished. You must divorce the thoughts from your mind that lead you to believe that there is a limited supply of whatever it is that you want, and that only the more fortunate people are the ones who get it. You must set your gaze in the direction you want to go. Stop envying the people who live the life you wish you could and be happy for them as you would want others to be happy for your successes. You can't measure all of your success on material things, but you can always measure your success by your level of happiness that you feel you have. And just like happiness, both poverty and abundance are a state of mind. And based on your current belief you are now choosing which state you're living in. However, do know that poverty is the default state when you are crippled by fear.

Symptoms include:

- *Indifference*. Commonly expressed through lack of ambition; willingness to tolerate poverty; acceptance of whatever compensation life may offer without protest; mental and physical laziness; lack of initiative, imagination, enthusiasm and self-control.
- *Indecision*. The habit of permitting others to do one's thinking. Staying "on the fence." Unwilling to commit to doing something that may fail or cause embarrassment.
- *Doubt*. Generally expressed through alibis and excuses designed to cover up, explain away, or apologize for one's failures, sometimes expressed in the form of envy of those who are successful, or by criticizing them. Other times expressed as pretending to know more about something than what is actually known.
- *Worry*. Usually expressed by finding fault with others, a tendency to spend beyond one's means, neglect of personal appearance, scowling and frowning; intemperance in the use of alcohol, drugs, or other addictive substances; nervousness, lack of poise and self-consciousness. Worry is also exhibited as being suspicious of other people's motives without foundation. Physical symptoms include digestive issues, excessive perspiration, dry mouth, wringing of the hands, facial tics, and involuntary muscle movements.

- *Over-caution*. The habit of looking for the negative side of every circumstance thinking and talking of possible failure instead of concentrating on the means of succeeding. Knowing all the roads to disaster, but never searching for the plans to avoid failure. Waiting for "the right time" to begin putting ideas and plans into action until the waiting becomes a permanent habit. Remembering those who have failed and forgetting those who have succeeded. Seeing the hole in the doughnut but overlooking the doughnut. Pessimism, leading to indigestion, poor elimination, autointoxication, bad breath and bad disposition. Over-caution is oftentimes linked with being indecisiveness. To avoid making a mistake, one will overthink something to the point of becoming immobilized. And avoiding making mistakes is the over-caution person's primary mission in life.

- *Procrastination*. The habit of putting off until tomorrow that which should have been done a year ago. Spending too much time in creating alibis and excuses for not completing the job. This symptom is closely related to over-caution, because it also contains the ingredients of doubt and worry. Refusal to accept responsibility whenever it can be avoided. Willingness to give-up or compromise rather than put up a tough fight. Discounting challenges instead of harnessing and using them as stepping-stones to achievement. Bargaining with life for a penny instead of demanding prosperity, opulence, abundance, contentment and happiness. Unwillingness to put a mental plan in place of what to do when overtaken by failure. Hanging on to a miserable condition instead of burning all bridges behind and thereby making retreat impossible. Weakness of, and often total lack of self-confidence, definiteness of purpose, self-control, initiative, enthusiasm, ambition, thrift and sound reasoning ability. Expecting poverty instead of demanding wealth. Association with those who accept poverty instead of seeking the company of those who demand and obtain wealth.

Most of these symptoms can be applied to other fears as well. However, for those who have wealth, these symptoms may not appear to be so obvious, or they may manifest themselves in slightly different ways. Having wealth does not render one immune to fear. I had a friend who was quite well off financially, however she was ravaged with many fears, including the fear of one day possibly losing most or all of her money. She became so miserly that she would not shop for new clothing even when her old clothes were showing signs of wear and tear. By the way, she is the friend that introduced me to thrift shops. But I like to shop at thrift stores not because I'm cheap, but because its fun looking at all the things people throw out, and to find a "hidden" treasure every now and then. You might say that the difference between she and I was that I was rich with a little bit of money, and she was poor with a lot of money. So, as you can surmise, she had a fear of poverty even though she wasn't impoverished. One's background on how they were raised to think about money can have a profound effect on a person their entire lifetime. If you haven't done so already, refer to **Appendix B** in the back of this book and answer the questions as best you can to see what your relationship to money is all about. Primarily those who fear the loss of their wealth do not see money as either an expression of themselves, or as a medium of exchange. They treat money as a child who carries around a security blanket. And that's not to say that having a sufficient amount of money doesn't bring a level of comfort to your mind in knowing that you have spending power and that you can honor your financial obligations. But it is to say that feeling secure is a state of mind that is produced when the subconscious mind supplies the conscious mind with the knowledge of who you truly are. And the subconscious knows exactly what the conscious mind needs to experience knowing.

## Public Enemy #2 – The Fear of Criticism

This fear, as it pertains to finances, is believed by some behavioral scientists to be based on a perceived societal pressure of "keeping up with the Jones". As one comedian said, people go out and buy things they don't need; with money they don't have; to impress people they don't like. The fearful person believes that if they do this then they won't be criticized. That criticism will fall on the person who is not doing it. To them who possess this fear it represents their incompetence, stupidity, uncouthness, perversity, and lack of substance as a significant person. So, as you can see, it can go beyond the acquisition of money alone, and is at the heart of being afraid of losing one's reputation. Particularly if they take pride in their reputation that they believe others see them as someone to be highly regarded. It's the reason why some people belong to a religious persuasion and base their "goodness" on their regular attendance. Their reasoning is that a person who is classified as "good" cannot be characterized or criticized as being a "bad" person. Another reason why people have this fear is because they associate criticism with consequences and repercussions. Perhaps while growing up their parent(s) criticized them first for either not having done something they were told to do or having done something that was considered unsatisfactory and it was followed with punitive measures. So, the fear remains for those who believe punishment will follow, or that if they are criticized then they deserve to be punished. And if you look at some of the events in history where people who were criticized most, they suffered at the hands of their respective societies. The absurdity of it is capricious and arbitrary. Case in point, what about a women who goes out with a man, and he buys her drinks, he buys her dinner, he may even buy her flowers; if she decides to have sex with him at the end of the date, hardly anyone would criticize her behavior. However, if he goes to her place and she takes money from him and allows him to have sex with her, then she is not only subjected to be criticized, but also could face criminal charges for solicitation. The "date" produces the same result, but how the result was established is subjective to people's opinions.

## You're the Best Thing that Ever Happened to Me!

It has been said that we are our own biggest critic, and I believe that statement is fairly accurate when we have internalized the myths, misconceptions, and misguided advice from others about ourselves. Then we naturally begin to criticize ourselves. We somehow try to believe that we can do better than our best in any given moment. You may know, going into a situation that you are unwilling to totally committing yourself to do your best, however the fact remains that how you acted in that situation was the best you were willing to give. Even after a situation is completed and you take the time to analyze how you think it went, then you certainly may come up with something that you might have done differently. But you don't have the luxury of hindsight during the event, only after. Again, you gave it the best you had in that moment, at which point criticism serves no useful purpose. But what about constructive criticism, you ask. Well, there is no such thing as constructive criticism. That's an oxymoron to link the words constructive and criticism together. It's like jumbo shrimp. There is nothing jumbo about a shrimp. And there is nothing constructive about criticism. If someone is in a position to evaluate your performance, if they want to offer you something constructive, it must come in the form of suggestions and/or recommendations. Because the very nature of criticism is to put-down, not to build up. Self-criticism that leads to self-loathing is the fastest most effective way to reach low self-esteem than by any other means. Because if you can't think highly of yourself, how could you expect others to do so? The attitude you hold about yourself is reflected in your mannerisms of which most people can detect, particularly if they are around you frequently. That's why it is imperative that you think most highly of yourself because most people don't want to associate themselves with someone who thinks he is a loser unless they think of themselves in that way also.

## The Saga of Little Miss Perfect

Being criticized is the perfectionist worst nightmare because Little Miss Perfect's world is built on appearances. She does not want to be scrutinized by others and then criticized for not being able to get it "right" every time, especially the first time. She is a people pleaser and resents that she is. So, she oftentimes spends her time alone trying to stay under the radar and moving about with minimum detection. This fear of criticism causes her much anxiety because the thought of someone asking her to do something that she may not be able to pull off, is never far away in her mind. And she spends too much time and energy thinking about what might happens, and not enough time thinking about what can happen if she looked at the irrationality of her fear and let it go. If she continues to hold onto this state of mind, she will lose all sense of self by allowing others to define her self-worth. Little Miss Perfect may develop a condition call obsessive-compulsive disorder. This means she becomes highly methodical and systematic in an attempt to control her environment. The obsession is her state of mind based on her perception that she needs to be extremely organized. She thinks this will help her control the chaos she oftentimes experiences with her thoughts. It is a deep-seated belief that if her surroundings are not orderly, then she will become disoriented and confused and thereby rendering her out-of-control and inefficient. And thereafter getting criticized for letting things get out of hand. So, the compulsion is in her actions to create and maintain a highly stable predictable environment that will help her cope with the chaos that she perceives in others and attempts to minimize in herself. There are times when Little Miss Perfect will take a risk in an attempt to do something that she hasn't done before, but it is a most highly calculated risk where she perceives that she can be perfect at it. She may even be competitive in certain areas where her skills are matched against others, because she carries the expectation of coming out on top or very near the top. Which she perceives as another way of silencing her critics, because who can openly criticize a winner? She may even show signs of sympathizing with the losers, but she is almost impervious of feeling empathy toward others. Until she comes to the realization that it doesn't matter whether she live with a little chaos in her life, or if she choose to live a highly organized one, the main goal is to be happy and content with yourself irrespective of what others think, say, or do.

## Would You Rather Have Broken Bones?

As a child my friends and I would say, "sticks and stones can break my bones, but words can never hurt me". Well, that's not all together true, words do hurt, particularly when they come from people you care about. But it takes the mature mind to feel the hurt, and then move on. But as children we operate primarily on our feelings because our mind is still in the developmental stage of trying to understand how to analyze, categorize, and utilize information. So, criticism to children can penetrate to their core especially when it is done in a mean-spirited way. Granted, no criticism is good, but some people criticize because they think they are helping the person, as opposed to those who criticize for the purpose of belittling them. And when criticism has pierced someone to the core, it becomes difficult for them to build their self-esteem unless they receive counter remarks that they can build on. It has been noted that it takes more than a dozen kind remarks to offset one disparaging remark said to a child. Much of a child's self-esteem is built around their awareness of their level of importance to the adults in their lives. And people who suffer from the fear of criticism probably developed it in early childhood through the relationships they had with the adults in their lives. That's not to say that adults are the sole contributing factor of this fear, because peers can also be less than kind. And during the formative years of a child's self-perception they can become so self-conscious of their "faults" that it results in the creation of a poor self-image.

I'll list here the seven major symptoms Mr. Hill considered to be caused by the fear of criticism including their definitions. Do a self-examination and see if any of these symptoms apply to you.

- *Self-consciousness.* Generally expressed through nervousness, timidity in conversation and in meeting strangers, awkward movement of the hands and limbs, shifting of the eyes. An overall uneasiness displayed from feeling uncomfortable in one's own body.

- *Lack of poise*. Expressed through lack of voice control, nervousness in the presence of others, especially strangers, poor posture of body, poor memory.
- *Bland Personality*. Lacking in firmness of decision-making, personal charm, and ability to express opinions definitively. The habit of sidestepping issues instead of meeting them head on. Agreeing with others without carefully examining their opinions and the motives behind them.
- *Inferiority complex*. The habit of expressing self-approval by word of mouth and by actions, as a means of covering up a feeling of inferiority. Usually by bragging or boasting about themselves. Using big words to impress others (often without knowing the real meaning of the words). Having no originality of their own they will imitate others in dress, speech and mannerisms. Boast of imaginary achievements and/or "name dropping" in an attempt to be associated with someone considered to be important.
- *Extravagance*. The habit of overspending in an attempt to impress others with what they own.
- *Lack of initiative*. Failure to embrace opportunities for self-advancement, fear of expressing their opinions with any authority, lack of confidence in their own ideas, giving evasive answers to questions asked by their superiors or supervisors, hesitancy of manner and speech, deceit in both words and deeds.
- *Lack of ambition*. Mental and physical laziness, lack of self-assertion, indecisiveness and slowness in reaching decisions, being too easily influenced and dissuaded by others, the habit of criticizing others behind their backs and flattering them to their faces, the habit of accepting defeat without protest or quitting an undertaking when opposition by others seem too foreboding, suspicions of others without cause, lack of tactfulness of manner and speech, unwillingness to accept the responsibility for mistakes that are made.

The fear of criticism is also closely related to the fear of disappointment. Some people fear that if they attempt something new and fail at it, the disappointment would be devastating. To avoid being disappointed they simply refuse to take risks even when the benefit could be great. I had a patient who wanted to go into real estate. She didn't fear failing the real estate exam as much as she did thinking that she wouldn't make any sales after she got her license. And the investment in real estate school and taking the exam would have all been for naught in her own mind and devastating to her confidence. The truth of the matter was that she already lacked self-confidence in her ability to do something she thought she would enjoy doing. Many people self-sabotage their desires because they fear being disappointed if things don't work out. They may even go so far as to make a plan and talk to their significant others about their desire, and then at the last minute they fold their tent and limp back to the familiar. Because the familiar doesn't disappoint them, it gives them the same old crap that they are used to. Disappointments are a part of the mystery of life. When one learns to become friends with disappointment then they understand that within every failed attempt lies the seed of opportunity that turns that attempt into an object lesson to learn and grow from.

## Public Enemy #3 – The Fear of ill Health

There is a widespread belief that when you get old, you lose your health. And this belief has created fear of both aging and debilitated health as a result. And the premiere fear that encompasses both of these fears is the fear of death. But we can single out the fear of ill health from the other two because many people fear it while still in their prime. Not only is the pharmaceutical industry capitalizing on this, but also the vitamin supplement industry. People run to their doctor to get pills prescribed, and to the health food stores to get some supplement they feel they need because they aren't getting enough of what their body needs from their diet. Most people would probably not admit to having this fear of ill health, because they tell themselves and others that their actions are based on trying to live healthy. But the truth is, a healthy lifestyle does not come in a bottle. And there is some truth that suggests that most people eat far too much processed foods that are deficient in some nutrients that the body needs. And of course, when one is sick, they should take their medication. But what Mr. Hill and I are suggesting is that the fear of ill health is producing more imaginary illnesses and poor health choices than what naturally occurs when the body declines in its youthful vigor. The old saying, "You're only as old as you feel", would be great to hear from time-to-time if it didn't come with the stipulation, "And in order to feel and look younger you need this product that you can receive with our exclusive offer of just $19.99", as the infomercials would have you believe. And it's not that I'm against taking supplements because I take them myself, but at specific times for specific reasons. During the winter months I take a vitamin C and D supplement, and during the summer months I take B-12. But I don't think for a second that if I weren't taking these that my health would start to deteriorate overnight.

Over the past few decades there have been several studies conducted on psychosomatic disorders. These are illnesses reported by patients to their doctors of symptoms they perceive themselves to be having. The thought of being ill can come from either a suggestion from someone else, such as "Are you feeling alright, because you don't look so good?"; or it can come from an autosuggestion when you say things to yourself such as, "I wonder what's wrong with me, I don't feel like myself anymore these days.". After deciding that they aren't feeling well, some people go on-line and visit one of the medical websites. First of all, let me say that I believe most of the medical website can be very useful. However, these websites can also be the reason why people start to think themselves sick because they look at a sickness and its symptoms, and suddenly the person believes they are experiencing these very symptoms and therefore must be sick. Because the fear of illness can and will attract illnesses toward you.

Your mind is so powerful, and as was aforementioned about autosuggestions, they can work on positive suggestions or negative ones; so, the more your fear of illness prompts you to think about becoming sick will cause your mind to go into the production of it. So, if you don't want to get sick, then stop telling yourself, "I think I must be coming down with something", whenever you get a sniffle.

Some of the symptoms of the fear of illness include:

- *Autosuggestion*. The habit of negative use of self-suggestion by looking for and expecting to find the symptoms of all kinds of illnesses and/or diseases. The secondary benefit of being ill is receiving the sympathy from others, so the imagined illness allows the person to "enjoy" being sick. The habit of trying all sorts of so-called remedies, potions, fad diets, and gimmicks recommended by others as having medicinal or therapeutic value. Talking to others about operations, accidents and other forms of illness. Experimenting with "health" diets, physical exercises, weight-reducing systems, without professional guidance or thorough research before commencing.
- *Hypochondria*. (A medical term meaning imaginary illness) The habit of talking about illness, concentrating the mind on diseases, and expecting it to appear. Subjecting one's self to going from one illness to another depending on which one is talked about most at the time. In addition to physical illnesses and diseases, hypochondriacs can also create mental illnesses for themselves such as nervous breakdowns, depression, and high anxiety.
- *Lack of Proper Exercise*. Fear of ill health can lead to the avoidance of maintaining healthy exercise habits that can result in obesity, muscle atrophy, low energy levels, and risks of coronary and heart disease. Lack of proper exercise may also affect one's ability to sustain REM sleep (Rapid Eye Movement, considered to be essential for deep sleep).
- *Susceptibility*. The fear of ill health breaks down the natural

resistance in the body and creates a favorable condition for any form of disease one may contract. In other words, the auto-immune system becomes compromised to the point of not being able to ward-off germs that cause illnesses.

- *Self-pity.* The individual who uses this trick does so not only to make themselves feel bad, but to illicit the sympathy of others. If they are not truly a hypochondriac, they may feign an illness to lure others into feeling sorry for them. They may use an imaginary illness as a means to cover-up their sheer laziness, or to serve as an excuse or an alibi for their lack of ambition.

- *Intemperance.* The habit of using alcohol or other addictive substances to alleviate pain, both real and imaginary, instead of addressing the cause of the so-called pain. Most hypochondriacs use several medications at the same time, and most believe they will die if they were to stop taking all the pills. Those who get addicted to non-prescription drugs and alcohol also do so as a means of trying to cope with their fear of illness, and oftentimes their fear of loneliness and of death. The habit of constantly reading about illness and worrying over the possibility of being stricken by it. The habit of ordering every advertised health aid that promises "improved" health. Some individuals who have this fear of illness go to extremes in their exercise routine. They literally become "gym-rats" and use exercise as a means to stave-off illness. While exercise is a good source of maintaining good muscle tone and cardio-vascular health, when the body isn't allowed to recover from strenuous workouts, it can cause the body more harm than good.

# Public Enemy #4 – The Fear of Loss of Love

Suffice it to say, this is the most painful of all the six fears because it threatens what we all want most, love. And this fear may indeed be the oldest fear experienced by mankind. Based on the assumption that man is polygamous by nature, and man's track-record of sexual exploits shows strong indications that he is. During man's earliest years on the planet he developed a behavior of stealing his fellow-man's mate and taking liberties with her whenever he could. This is believed to be the primary reason why jealousy and other similar forms of neurosis grew out of man's inherited fear of the loss of love of someone. Back during the stone age, men would steal females by the use of brute force. And during the dark and middle ages, men would take women as wives, concubines, and slaves whenever they conquered another tribe or nation. The act of stealing females still goes on today, men just use different techniques. Instead of brute force, they now use persuasion, the promise of giving her things that she likes, fine cars, clothing, and other "bait" which is much more effective than physical force. Man's attitudes and behaviors toward women are pretty much the same as they were at the dawn of civilization, but man expresses them differently. Even though the U.S. has experienced some needed changes in how women are treated in the workplace, still the number one crime against women in the world today is rape and sexual assault. Some may argue that rape is not about sexual intercourse, but about exerting power and domination over another person. I can't disagree with that. However, I will contend that men have done and are still doing much to try to control how women are allowed to express their sexuality. Look at prostitution, it's a form of controlling what a woman can do with her body. If the truth be told, the large majority of men are probably for the legalization of it, but societal pressure prohibits them from admitting it openly. Especially when it's cloaked in the garb of being morally indecent. But, from the White House to the whorehouse, men have engaged in extramarital affairs since time began. The Mormons seem to grasp and acknowledge this about male behavior and incorporate it in their system of beliefs, as does other cultures around the world. But this is not a treatise on male sexual behavior, it's just part of an explanation of how the fear of losing love came about. However, women seem to be more susceptible to this fear than men. This could also date back to women's experiences with men throughout history. Women have learned, whether they want to openly admit it or not, that men are basically polygamous by nature, and that they are not to be trusted in the hands of rivals. By the way, this does not suggest that women aren't or can't be polygamous. If you look in the animal kingdom, it is the female in many species that will copulate with many males in order to ensure her eggs get fertilized. It is natures' way of propagating the species.

The distinguishing symptoms of this fear are:

- *Jealousy*. The habit of being suspicious of friends and loved ones without provocation or any reasonable evidence of sufficient grounds. The habit of making accusations of infidelity against your spouse or significant other without evidence. The habit of attempting to control your spouses or significant others' whereabouts, to "keep tabs" on them so they don't wander astray. Having a general suspicion of everyone, demonstrating having no faith in anyone.
- *Fault finding*. The habit of pointing out the faults in other people without the slightest provocation, or without any cause whatsoever.
- *Back-stabbing*. The habit of talking about people in a less than kind manner outside of their presence.
- *High-risk taking*. The habit of performing destructive behaviors that carry a higher than average risk factor. This includes behaviors such as, gambling, stealing, cheating, and otherwise taking hazardous chances to provide money for loved ones, with the belief that love can be bought. Or seeking to gain notoriety for "beating the odds" and believing that other will think highly of them for doing so. The habit of spending beyond one's means, or incurring an exorbitant amount of debt, to provide gifts for loved ones, with the objective of making a favorable impression. Other symptoms may include:

Insomnia, nervousness, lack of persistence, weakness of will, lack of self-control, lack of self-reliance, and having a bad temper.

- *Making threats*. The habit of telling one's spouse or significant other that they will either cause them physical harm, or they will do physical harm to themselves if their partner every leaves them. Or they will threaten to ruin their spouses' or significant other's reputation; or threaten them with financial ruin if they decide to ever depart from the relationship. If children are involved, they will threaten to take the children away.

## The Love I Lost

No one wants to lose love. And the truth of the matter is that you can't. Granted there are emotions people have that they interpret as love, but love goes beyond emotional feelings alone. I like the way the Apostle Paul describe some of the characteristics of love in 1 Corinthians 13 in the Christian bible, my interpretation of what he says is that love is patient, love is kind, love is not envious, it is not egotistical, does not behave itself in an unfair manner that take advantage of others, is not quick to pass judgment, doesn't think evil thoughts about people, finds no pleasure in other's misfortunes, but rejoices in their successes. Love accepts all things for what they are, it hopes for the best in every situation, and it accepts other's rights to decide for themselves. And Love <u>never</u> fails. So, love is not something that you can lose because love is not something that you can give to someone, love is the essence of who you are. You can however express the qualities of love that are in you with others. And as you can see, the descripts of love is primarily based on what it is known not to be rather than what it is. Because love defies all human definitions and reasonings for its existence. In other words, love is greater than mankind, even though every person is affected by it.

When people leave us that we care about, whether through

changing local, divorce, or death, it is not uncommon to feel the void of their absence. But love is a spiritual thing, and you can continue loving a person even in absentia. But on the other hand, if you feel anger toward them after their departure, you might want to question whether you truly loved this person at all or did their leaving trigger your fear of abandonment. As children we are bonded to others primarily by our feelings. But as we mature, we start to cultivate our relationships with practices that support our affection toward them. And when you get to the state of mind where you recognize that the bond between you and another is bound by something greater than the both of you, then you can begin to understand the significance of the statement, Perfect Love cast out *all* fear.

## Public Enemy #5 – The Fear of Old Age

This fear is most subtle in that it sneaks up on the person who begins to realize that they have a diminished capacity to do some of the things they use to do quite easily. The fear is not limited to diminished physical prowess alone, but also diminished mental acuity. Some people equate old age with senility, Alzheimer's, Parkinson's disease, and other forms of dementia. While it is true that the onset of mental deterioration does occur in old age, it can also occur earlier in life. Such things as concussions, heavy alcohol and drug use, and disease can cause diminished brain functioning. The fear of old age may also be associated with the belief that one might lose their independence if they become incapacitated to the point of not being able to take care of their basic needs. Being taken away from their home and placed in an assisted-living facility or nursing home can drive this fear. Secondly, this fear can derive from the belief that when one loses their youthfulness, then they become sexually unattractive. This applies to both men and women, however it has more of an effect on men who believe that woman find physical attractiveness in men as their first priority for wanting to be with a man. This may be true for most men, but not for most women. Studies have shown that a woman's desire to be with a man is primarily prompted by her intuition that sees him as having certain potentials. That potential can cover many different areas, from perceiving a man as potentially being a good provider, a good companion, a good parent, a good lover, etc. Also, some women's sex drive is highly diminished after menopause mainly because of a lower estrogen level. Men's testosterone level decreases as he gets older, but this has more of an effect on his performance more so than his desire for sex. In other words, the spirit may be willing, but the flesh is, well you get the point.

Mr. Hill states that there are two very sound reasons for man's apprehension of old age. One is that man distrusts his fellowman who he believes will seize his possessions if he does not have the capacity to protect them. This fear dates back to the stone age when the only protection man had for his "stuff", including his woman, was himself. And secondly, that he is headed to a terrible place he pictures in his mind as the world beyond of which he is totally unfamiliar with. This fear also dates back to a time when man did not think in abstract terms. What he saw was what he would attach a meaning to that he could understand. And since he could not see beyond the grave, his fear was that it must not offer him anything worthwhile since he himself killed in order to survive. So, the insurance companies capitalize on the first fear of losing one's possessions. And the religious institutions capitalize on the second fear of speculating about what goes on after one dies.

The most common of the symptoms of the fear of old age are:

- *Inferiority complex.* The tendency to slow down by thinking less of yourself as being competent. A tendency to believe that you are "slipping" and not as mentally sharp or physically virile as you once were. Believing that life is about winning and losing, you begin to identify yourself with the "losers" because of your age. The tendency to believe that you are expendable and not needed or respected by others. The fear of loneliness can come into play when one has an inferiority complex that tells them they are unloved and unlovable.

- *Cynical.* The tendency to distrust the sincerity or integrity of others. Therefore, the person who possess this fear will oftentimes speak apologetically of themselves as a means of blaming their age; as opposed to expressing gratitude for having reached the age of wisdom and understanding. You may have heard of or experienced being around a crotchety "old" person who shows little to no gratitude for what others do for them. That's because they are angry because they can't do it themselves, or they believe the person who does something for them does so because they have a hidden agenda. The person with this fear can also become very sarcastic and mean spirited when they feel envious of others.
- *Apathetic.* The tendency to develop the habit of killing off initiative, imagination, and self-reliance by falsely believing they are too old to exercise these qualities. The tendency to not care too deeply or not care at all about things that should be of concern because they have a direct effect on their life.
- *Pathetic.* The tendency to become time-warped back to a time when life was supposedly at its best. This person will wear clothing they believe will make them appear younger. They may even adopt a vocabulary containing words that young people may use when communicating with their peers, thereby inspiring ridicule by both friends and strangers.

## Eat, Drink, and Be Merry, for Tomorrow We All Die!

Some people think that you age as time progresses. Whereas time does have an effect on the aging process as chronology is used, but the truth of the matter is, we don't age, our cells do. Our bodies are made up of cells that form our organs and conduct their activity. The millions of cells in our bodies are composed of many atoms. When healthy these atoms replicate themselves and keeps the cells healthy which contributes to the body's overall health, youthfulness, and free from disease. What makes an atom healthy is that it has paired electrons, which acts pretty much like a sperm and egg. However, atoms that are missing an electron is what causes it to be unhealthy. Not only that, these unhealthy atoms act as a destroyer of good atoms by "stealing" their electrons. An atom missing an electron is call a Free Radical, which alter or destroy healthy cells. Cells that die, and cells that replicate in a damaged state are the cause of or contribute to premature aging, sicknesses and diseases such as cancer, heart disease, osteoporosis, and many others. Some of the primary culprits that are responsible for creating Free Radicals are: smoking, stress, excessive sunlight, pesticides used in growing foods, air pollution, some medications, food additives, x-rays, excessive chlorine in treated water, mercury in seafood, and many others. Now before you get totally rattled and think that you're doomed, keep in mind that your body does produce antioxidants that fight and destroy Free Radicals. However, you can assist your body by taking certain measure to avoid things you can control. And as your mother use to tell you, "eat your (organic) vegetables.". So, eat, drink, and be merry in a responsible way, and tomorrow you might not die.

Someone said that we stop laughing when we get old. But actually, the reverse is true, we get old when we stop laughing. Because laughter is indeed the best medicine there is. So, make sure you take heavy doses as often as possible. And take some sound advice from the popular song sang by Bobby McFerrin, "Don't Worry, Be Happy".

## Public Enemy Number 6 - The Fear of Death

This fear is thought to be the cruelest of all the basic fears. The primary reason is because for thousands of years people have been scared senseless into believing that death is the end of the road for "getting things right with God". You could probably conclude that so-called non-believers are probably less afraid of death than those who claim to believe in a god who demands a strict code of conduct to avoid a painful afterlife. Of all the mysteries, death holds the greater because there is no way of knowing what death truly is until you die.

And there have been accounts of people who have had near-death experiences where they reported that they could either enter into the spirit realm or return to their human existence. And there have also been reports by those who believe they died in one life and was reincarnated into another. Some say they've done this hundreds of times. There are some who believe the soul is immortal and therefore after death it simply returns to the spirit world from whence it came. Who can undisputedly claim any of these accounts are false? There's certainly no way of knowing for sure, until it happens to you. But the fear of death is based on being so afraid of the unknown to the point that one cannot fully enjoy the benefits of living.

## Now I Lay Me Down to Sleep

I recall as a child starting off all of my prayers with, now I lay me down to sleep, I pray thee Lord my soul to keep. If I should die before I wake, I pray thee Lord my soul to take. I didn't really know the import of what I was saying, but it was a cute little rhyme and it got me started in talking to what I believed was God. It never was a conversation between God and me, I was more or less asking God to bless me and my family. But as I got older, I became more aware through my religious upbringing that life was all about doing the "right" things. Which of course was dictated by the good people who designated themselves as God's spokespersons. And they could back it up because they had the bible, for god sake. So, at some point I developed this fear of death because I wasn't sure if I was always doing the "right" things. I tried to, and I was pretty sure I succeeded often in being a "good" boy. But I just wasn't sure if it was enough to keep me out of Hell's Kitchen. I don't recall when it was that I had my break with this concept of eternal damnation for those who weren't pleasing to a god who demanded absolute righteousness, and most of all justice. But I do recall that it set me free and I was able to live my life as a person who believed in doing the "right" thing because it was "right" to me, and not because there were eternal consequences if I didn't. The point of my little story is that children can be traumatized early in life and unable to be fully happy with themselves when fears loom overhead, especially the fear of death. Some children never get over it, and they develop all manner of neurotic and superstitious behaviors as a result. Because the fear of death paralyzes one's reasoning ability to look at it from both an objective and subjective way.

## Physics 101

As I mentioned, I don't recall just when it hit me that eternal damnation with fire and brimstone awaiting the damned became metaphorical rather than actual, but perhaps it was sometime during my college years. Because college cause you to think and question things and indulge your curiosities. Well, we learn in elementary physics that the world is made up entirely of two substances, energy and matter. Based on this knowledge is the fact that neither of these two substances can be created or destroyed. Both can be transformed but not destroyed. Life is energy, if it is anything. Our bodies are composed of matter and needs the supply of energy to move about. This energy is your Lifeforce, or life source, or life substance. Even your thoughts are transformers of energy. That's how you are able to personally move matter. So, if neither energy nor matter can be destroyed, then life cannot be destroyed. Life, like other forms of energy, may go through various stages of transformation and transition, but it cannot be destroyed. So, that would mean that death is nothing more than a transition of the energy of life. And if death is nothing more than a change, or transition, then nothing comes after death except an eternal peaceful sleep; or you could call it an unconsciousness of that which you are capable of being conscious of now. You may ask, but what happens to my consciousness? Consciousness is your awareness of your environment, put another way, it is *your* current reality. Therefore, when you die, you won't be conscious of yourself as yourself in your current reality, but you may be conscious of yourself in a different reality. Because your new environment will change and you will be aware of whatever changed environment your sub-conscious mind, or spirit, leads you to. Your spirit is life, which is the energy that transforms itself as it deems appropriate according to the law of natural order. Most religious communities support this idea, but perhaps not in the manner that it was just presented. However, the belief that there is life after death is a tenet of every major religion.

## The Circle of Life

In the Broadway play, The Lion King, the father explains the re-lationship between the lions and the antelopes to his son. He tells him that although the lions' prey upon the antelope for food, when the lions dies, their bodies are transformed to help in the process of growing grass, which the antelope eat for food. Thus, they are both a part of the circle of life. This should tell you something about how life works. It would serve no purpose in the circle of life to have anyone burning forever in some cosmic bonfire. Life is a self-perpetuating evolving entity, and nothing goes to waste or is relegated to a useless purpose. You might say that life is very efficient when it comes to re-cycling. So, the next time you go to a memorial service for someone, know that they truly are in a better place.

Some of the symptoms associated with the fear of death are:

- *Paranoia*. The tendency to deem most unfamiliar situations requiring physical participation as potentially life threatening and thereby choosing to avoid them. The tendency to think you are dying when you become ill or when you are around illness. The tendency to take the latest "Wonder Drug" in an attempt to stave off death. The tendency to believe that others want you dead.
- *Superstition*. The tendency to perform certain rituals that are believed to ward off death. Church going can certainly be classified as one of these rituals when it is done as a means of striking a bargain with God. You go to church, then God doesn't kill you.

- *Controlling*. This is closely related to both paranoia and superstition in that you seek to control your environment by eliminating any and all things that reminds you of your own mortality.
- *Religious fanaticism*. The tendency to use religion as a means of trying to convince others that you are right as it pertains to knowing what God likes and dislikes, and that they "ought to" believe the same as you do. The underlying bases for this, is that you think if everyone agrees with your beliefs then it makes it right. It's an attempt to create righteousness by consensus. Religious fanatics are driven by this fear of death and go to great lengths to perform their ritualistic behaviors. This may include browbeating other people into submission by telling them what to believe.
- *Emotional vacancy*. The fear of death robs you of seeking your true purpose in life. By that I mean, you have tucked away in your subconscious mind the idea that life can be over at any given moment. Therefore, you don't perceive the many opportunities in life that you can take advantages of to enrich your life and add meaning and purpose to it. And without meaning and purpose, you become emotionally vacant because preparing for death consumes your thoughts and becomes the main focus of your life. It's not that you can't express emotions, you just don't have the ability to express the ones that are the most meaningful, like the expression of the joy of living.
- *Denial*. The tendency to avoid medical advice or attention when you are ill for fear that the diagnosis will reveal an incurable illness or disease. The tendency to engage in mind games that keeps you from dealing with what's actually ailing you.
- *Worry*. Worry is the means by which all fears are sustained. It is the habit of thinking into existence the worst-case scenario about entering into a situation of which you perceive

you have no control over. Like the joke about the man who was afraid of flying. He said he didn't fly because he feared he would be in an airplane crash. His friend told him that if it's not his time to die then it won't happen. He then retorted to his friend, "but what if it's the pilots time?". When you are consumed with worry, you don't realize how much of the excitement of living you are missing out on, because you worry about the result and fail to participate in the event.

## Que Sera Sera, Whatever Will Be, Will Be

When you think of worry, it is oftentimes overlooked as being the culmination of indecisions and the refusal to accept something that is for what it is. Mr. Hill says, "Relieve yourself, forever of the fear of death, by reaching a decision to accept death as an inescapable event. Whip the fear of poverty by reaching a decision to get along with whatever wealth you can accumulate without worry. Put your foot on the neck of the fear of criticism by reaching a decision not to worry about what other people think, do, or say. Eliminate the fear of old age by reaching a decision to accept it not as a handicap, but as a great blessing which carries with it wisdom, self-control, and understanding not known to youth. Acquit yourself of the fear of ill health by the decision to forget symptoms. Master the fear of loss of love by reaching a decision to get along without love, if that is necessary." All fears are learned through the acceptance of outside influences. Remember fear as the acronym – False Evidence Appearing Real. So, when you stop judging things by their appearances because they support your unsubstantiated beliefs, then you will see more clearly what the thing is that you're looking at. Worrying is a state of mind just like not worrying is a state of mind, but the choice is up to you as to which state you will live in. In order to rid yourself of the habit of worry, you must make an over-arching declaration that basically proclaims that nothing life presents to you is worth the price of worry. When this declaration is firmly implanted in your mind, it will bring you peace of mind, poise, and calmness of thought in your decision-making. And most of all it will increase the level of happiness you will experience on a regular basis.

## If at First You Don't Succeed, Try, Try, Again!

There are a couple of fears that Mr. Hill alluded to but did not name specifically that I think are relevant to look at a little bit closer. One is the fear of failure, which is associated with the fear of poverty. Because if you fail at being successful, then you will experience poverty. I don't necessarily mean the type of poverty where you are begging for coins on the street. But, the type of poverty that robs your spirit of the joy that comes from having made some accomplishments. I encounter this fear quite often when I counsel with college students who feel they are under a tremendous amount of pressure to succeed in their course studies in order to move on to the next phase, whether it's getting into a graduate school, or finding meaningful employment. The fear aspect motivates some to do their best in taking advantage of every resource the college has to offer that could improve their performance. While in others, the anxiety is so prevalent that they can hardly retain what they studied in preparation for an exam. Remember I said that fear can be a good motivator, but not a good teacher. So, even the ones who are motivated to put their study skill into overdrive are still subjected to high levels of distress that can have detrimental effects. But not all stress has debilitating effects. The good kind of stress is called eustress. This type of stress is like the adrenalin rush one gets when they know it's time to perform. This is caused by the excitement that one gets when they are about to engage in something that they feel they are prepared to meet the challenge. But for those who fear failure they cannot connect the dots that will give them a clear picture of a favorable outcome. When I counsel with students who experience this type of fear, I help them to look at life as a building process. Helping them to realize that they know more than they think they do, and that they are more than they use to be. We all are truly a work in progress, and the sooner we can accept that then we won't be so quick to judge ourselves and feed our fears. I believe this fear is associated with Attention Deficient Disorder (A.D.D.). The main reason for this connection is because the underlying fear of failure can impair one's ability to stay focused and become fidgety, and cause irritability. You may not think of this fear as being prevalent among adults, particularly when you live around people who appear to have "made it". But this fear is not restricted to finances only. Some people look at the divorce rate and it stirs the underpinning fear of a possible failed marriage for them.

## Success is Failure Turned Inside Out

I other fear I want to mention is on the same plain as the fear of failure, but it points in the opposite direction, it is the fear of success. Not many people if asked would own up to having this fear because of the stigma attached to it. That stigma being, who in their right mind would be afraid to achieve success? However, anyone who knows themselves to be living an unfulfilled life may suffer from it. This fear is the bases for this book, to help you overcome this fear so that you can apply the principles that's been laid out for you. Many people are afraid of success because success makes demands on your life. It requires that you take control of what you allow into your thoughts. It requires that you come up with a plan of action that will put you into a position of acquiring what you want most out of life. And it requires you to keep the flame of desire ablaze until you've reached your goals. This may sound difficult, but it really isn't. And I've purposely made this statement toward the end of the book so that you will see that you have already started the process each time you read about something and it held your attention. Think of all the nonsensical thoughts you've previously allowed to flood into your mind that profited you nothing. Or the get rich quick schemes you've entertained or even sought after that inevitably lead you down that long dark corridor of disappointment. Or how long did it take for you to accept your life as being mediocre? When did it become so enticing for you to sit in the middle of your comfort-zone and not push yourself to new heights? How many times have you kicked yourself for not having done something that you later felt was the right opportunity? When were you convinced that the words "I Can't" should be a significant part of your vocabulary?

## Thank You Falettinme Be Myself, Again

Your comfort zone is the place where your feelings like to hang out. It's the place where you feel the least disturbed and bothered by things that are unfamiliar. Your comfort zone affords you the pleasure of basically doing nothing out of the ordinary, which means that it is not demanding in any way, especially when you remain right in the center of it. And one of the biggest things that I found that frightens many people from leaving the center of their comfort zone to venture out into uncharted territories of new behaviors, is their fear of failure. Again, to them, failure represents looking and feeling foolish for having tried something and failed. And looking foolish invites ridicule from others. And ridicule means you don't fit in because others don't approve of you. And if people disapprove of you, then something must be wrong with you. And if something is wrong with you then that means that people will not like you. And if people don't like you, then they certainly won't respect you. And if people don't respect you then you will lose your reputation. And if you lose your reputation, then you're nobody. And the beat goes on! So, as you can see, some people become literal prisoners of their comfort zone with a warden named *Insecurity*, and prison guards called *I Can't*. But, if you are to succeed in busting out of your cell, then you must become friends with failure. And to be honest with you, failure is not all that bad. It's a means of letting you know what not to do in many respects. Which in and of itself is a form of learning. When giving an example of this to my patients, I often refer to the story of Thomas Edison's quest to find a way for people to have light in a room without having to light candles or torches. Edison tried experiment after experiment that I'm sure some of his friends and colleagues might have said to him, "what the use man, give it up!". Had he listened to them he would have given up and you and I would probably be walking around with matches in our pockets. But after making roughly 10,000 experiments Mr. Edison got it right. All the previous experiments were simply ways of letting him know what not to do. You can do the same thing, it's just a matter of changing your perspective of what failure means. Or, eradicating the idea that it exists altogether. Because there is truth in the old saying that, "nothing beats a failure, but a try!". So as long as you keep trying . . .

## Feeling Alright?

This brings me to asking the question, "are you really sick and tired of being sick and tired of living without the things you want most?". Because you will not give up your current level of living until you no longer desire it. Even if it doesn't contribute to your overall happiness, you will continue to stick with it because it's familiar, and you want to think it makes you feel safe. Within the heart of your comfort zone you have established rituals and habits that you have grown familiar with and it gives you a sense of knowing what to reasonably expect. When you choose to remain at the center of your comfort zone, it limits your thinking about what things are possible, because it blocks out elements that are foreign or unknown to it. Also, because it gives you a false sense of security. This false sense of security is based on your perceived need and numerous attempts at minimizing your mistakes, which makes you look and feel foolish; or you are trying to please someone who you believe has a profound effect on your life. Ruling out the possibility of thinking independently about changing a situation that would require you to do something different; and thereby threaten your position to remain at the center of your comfort zone.

Living within your comfort zone is like living in a bubble, with you at the very center. But just because you have a comfort zone doesn't mean it can't be expanded. In order for this to happen, you have to move from the center of your bubble to the edges, because when you get to the edges of your comfort zone, you will discover that beyond the borders you established to keep things out, are opportunities that exist which previously you thought did not exist. The only thing that's holding you back is your fear of feeling uncomfortable. That is why some people procrastinate about doing things. Doing something different requires you to move away from the center of your comfort zone and become discomforted for a little while. But fear of not doing things "right" may cause you to do nothing at all. Because doing nothing at all is presumed to be better than doing something that makes you appear to look foolish or feel inadequate. Then there is the myth that you have plenty of time to do things in life, so you feel you can put something off until a more convenient time. Which is okay if you are putting something off in order to do something of more importance. That's called setting your priorities. But the procrastinator puts things off in favor of doing nothing and ends up feeling stressed when faced with time constraints to get other things done in addition to that which they put off. And that in many cases is what causes stress. And not necessarily the good kind of stress, eustress. But, rather distress. Granted some people work good under pressure, and if you are one of them, great! But, be willing to acknowledge when the fear of failure or the fear of success is getting in the way of you venturing out and doing something that may potentially awaken the sleeping giant within yourself.

# THE SIXTH SENSE – WISDOM'S DOORWAY

THE SIXTH SENSE is a term sometimes associated with paranormal phenomena, like having a vision of something before it happens. There was a movie made back in 1999 entitled The Sixth Sense, which depicted a young boy who had the ability to communicate with people who had died. This phenomenon basically acknowledges that the sixth sense is in-tune with the spirit realm. The sixth sense is also associated with the supernatural ability of a person to perceive things about someone's past or future that is tucked away somewhere in their mind. Usually psychics, shamans, medicine men, and others who believe they possess this supernatural ability to delve into people's past and future lives are considered unique individuals. However, according to Mr. Hill, every person has the ability to use their sixth sense as a means of acquiring the wisdom they need to possess whatever it is that they want. He describes it as the channel that Infinite Intelligence uses to voluntarily communicate with an individual without any effort from or demands by them. Mr. Hill believed that the sixth sense is incomprehensible to the individual who has not mastered the other twelve principles sited in this book. He says that without mastering these principles a person has no knowledge and no experience that they can use in comparison to the sixth sense. Mr. Hill states that in order to have access to the sixth sense it requires "meditation through mind development *from within*". Which simply means that you have to learn how to block out external chatter in order to listen to what's being communicated from within. Two primary benefits of being aware of the sixth sense is that in times of danger, it will give you warning, and when opportunities arise, it will notify you so that you may take full advantage of it.

## Miracle on 34<sup>th</sup> Street

Mr. Hill emphatically states that he doesn't believe in miracles. His reason for stating this is based on his statement that he believes that nature never deviates from the laws that govern it. He goes on to say that some of nature's laws are so incomprehensible that it sometimes produces what appears to be a miracle. This testimony is irrefutable if you take into consideration that every molecule down to the tiniest atom moves at the behest of Infinite Intelligence. And that everything in the Universe act in accordance to an intelligent order. And that every law that governs life moves knowledge and its expressions forward. Just like water will always flow to its lowest point when governed by the law of gravity. But what about when you pray for someone and they get better, isn't that a miracle being performed? I personally had this experience happen when I was around eight years old. I was vacationing with my grandmother at her mother's house in Arkansas where she was raised. I became very ill with chills, fever, and a tremendous amount of stomach discomfort. I was given medicines and potions to take, but nothing seemed to work. So, early one morning my grandmother bundled me up and took me down to the old well where she used to draw water as a girl and found solace to pray. She laid me down on a flattened log and moved about a stones' throw away from me and began to pray. Within seconds the place around me lit up like a Christmas tree and I was in awe of the brightness of the light. In fact, it was so radiant that it made everything appear translucent as if I could put my hand through solid objects. Well needless to say, the awesomeness of the experience I was having made me totally forget that I was sick. I jumped up off the log and ran over to my grandmother and asked her about the light. She said, "Baby, I didn't see a light, but are you feeling alright?", and I said yes, and she responded, "It was the Lord who came into this place and healed you.". Now, I'm not the only one who has experienced being healed by means of prayer. There have been many studies done in this area, and mostly all of them concur that prayer can make a difference in someone's physical health. Miracle or no? Well, going back to the principle that says where two or more are in harmony for achieving a desired result, Infinite Intelligence is in the midst. This is a law that governs how things from the invisible realm get manifested in the visible realm. Also realizing that there is an influence that humans have on each other at a deep level. Which is why New Thought pundits proclaim that we are all joined together by One Spirit which in essence is One Consciousness. If some people make you sick, then it stands to reason that others can make you well. I'm not about to make a determination for you, if you want to call it a miracle, then do so. And if you want to call it a natural law that governs the way life works, then call it that. The point is that the sixth sense is very much a part of your ability to comprehend certain things which the other five senses can't.

It is fundamental to man's nature to gravitate toward believing in something greater than himself. And it is believed by some behavioral scientists that it is the Sixth Sense that is responsible for this, considering it as the conduit between the spiritual realm and the physical realm. It reveals things to us that not only directs us toward our desires, but also provides the motivation for their attainment. The Sixth Sense only reveals to you that which you need to know in the present moment. It can be a revelation from some past event that you didn't know what that event meant at the time; or it can reveal something that is related to something that will happen in the future. It's like the phenomenon of déjà vu, when you have the experience of doing, or saying, or being someplace you feel like has happened before. The sixth sense reveals only as much as you need to know because to reveal too much before you are mentally ready to accept it, would hinder you from fully comprehending it. It's enough that you may oftentimes second guess it with your particular brand of logic after it has revealed something valuable to you. Don't forget, it doesn't care about nor uses your human logic or intellect to reveal accurate information you need to answer questions you may have about a given situation. Also, keep in mind that life has its up's and down's, which is nothing more than the rhythm of life. Everything in life moves by a certain rhythm. Even your own body has a biological process known as your circadian rhythm that lets you know what it wants, and the optimal times when it functions best. But the down's that comes with life aren't there to discourage you from continuing with your quest toward the attainment of your goals. The downs are there to help strengthen your resolve. As my grandmother use to say, "Whatever doesn't kill you, will help make you strong.". So, when the dark cloud of confusion seems to hover over you and you don't know what to do and want to give up, also remember that "The darkest hour is just before dawn!". And by staying the course, keeping the faith, you will experience a well-deserved change for the better.

As Mr. Hill states, "The sixth sense is not something that one can take off and put on at will.". If you are to use this mighty power, you must adhere to the principles presented in this book and use humility and gratitude as the basis for their implementation. Before you can become proficient at anything, you must practice it until it becomes second nature to you. You can say that the sixth sense works more efficiently with the disciplined mind. Because an undisciplined mind does not use valuable information in the same way as a disciplined mind does. It's no different than you shelling-out your hard-earned cash to someone who is responsible with money versus someone who is irresponsible with money. I'm not saying that you have to be so disciplined that you control every single thought that comes into your head. I'm saying that you must have a desire to discipline your mind and in so doing the sixth sense works with your mind in helping to develop the discipline it needs. This discipline isn't hard to achieve because it is your natural state of being. In other words, you learned to be undisciplined by the environment you were raised in. Remember I said that I still use the words, "may I", "thank you", and "please" without even thinking twice about it. And that's because the environment I was raised in promoted the use of these words on a consistent basis.

As children we are innately imbued with a desire to please our caregivers. There are exceptions that causes some children to exert their independence at an early age. I'm speaking from experience. My daughter Tracye was quite the recalcitrant child at a very young age. Doing things for the sake of pleasing others was not her thing. She did things on her own terms. Unlike her younger sister BryAnna, who seemed to enjoy pleasing others. It can come from genetics since young children are in the early stages of developing their social skills. But for those of us who did find comfort in knowing that we were doing what was expected of us by our caregivers, if they stressed something to us that we saw the value as pleasing them, then we were more likely to adopt it. This was how we disciplined our mind to adopt things we perceived as helpful, and discard things that we thought were a hinderance to pleasing our caregivers. I say caregivers because oftentimes there were authority figures that went beyond our parents, like grandparents. The culture I was raised in, gave the grandparents as much, if not more, authority than your parents had over you. If I misbehaved when I was with my grandparents, they didn't wait to tell my parents that I had misbehaved, discipline was meted out on the spot. Back then people acted on the belief that it takes a village to raise a child, and the children knew it and acted accordingly.

## Rewards and Punishments

As children, many people learned about disciplined through the rewards and punishment method. Most often the punishment for "bad" behavior was focused on more than receiving rewards for "good" behavior. That's because most children are expected to be "good"; good meaning, respectable, courteous, well-mannered, and grateful. And these qualities represented a well-disciplined child. On the other hand, an undisciplined child was considered to be a troublemaker. Because they lacked the discipline to control their emotions, they would usually resort to behaviors that drew undesirable attention to themselves. It more often was a cry for help but was treated as deserving of severe punishment. As time went by, the need for help began to increase for these undisciplined individuals and if they did not receive it their unruly behaviors became more extreme. Sometimes landing them in a prison cell. All because of a lack of self-discipline. I hope you can see now why I say that discipline is your natural state of being. It is something that we all need. Not just to do the "right" things according to societal standards and laws, but to do the most significant things that pertain to living a wholesome life.

You may have heard that the undisciplined mind is like a ship without a rudder, it has no means of getting you where you want to go. But a disciplined mind will carry you not only where you want to go but will get you there in as short a time as possible. Discipline is all about what you *choose* to practice. How you choose to practice what you practice is up to you. If the reward and punishment system work for you, then use it. However, I will caution you not to make the punishment too severe. For instance, if you have a report to write and a time restraint in which to write it, if you meet your deadline, then reward yourself with that second scoop of Ben and Jerrys. However, if you fail to meet your deadline, then you miss out on that second scoop of ice cream. But, DO NOT resort to self-condemnation because that will profit you nothing, in fact, it will only add insult to injury. Developing self-discipline require patience and an optimistic attitude. But, don't confuse patience with procrastination. Patience is moving forward after not having achieved a specific outcome with the understanding that there is something to be learned from that experience. Procrastination is telling yourself that you can put something off that needs to get done until a more convenient time. But there is never a more convenient time than right NOW!

## Star Light, Star Bright, The First Star
## I See Tonight, I WISH I May . . .

We've discussed the principles of "how to" obtain the things you desire most in life, and if followed you can't go wrong. However, they must be followed as a belief system and not as a wishful thinking approach. The difference being is that a belief system acknowledges that something that you set out to accomplish is already a foregone conclusion. In other words, it's already done, it's just a matter of following the steps to get there. Wishful thinking is having a desire but not knowing or even believing that it will be fulfilled. It's built on hope, which is needful, but with wishful thinking it stops there. In order to achieve what you want you must turn that hope into faith based on the belief that all the guiding principles and laws of life are all working in your best behalf. And your faith turns into a growing knowledge of your relationship to that which you desire. And that knowledge give you the capability to trust that your sixth sense will help get you there in the shortest amount of time. Because the sixth sense is the connecting point that directs the natural universal forces toward the desire you want manifested into your reality. In other words, the sixth sense is the agent the unconscious mind uses to bring all of the elements together to manifest your desires.

## It IS Finished!

There is a story in the Christian bible that says that God rested after the completion of creating the physical world. What I find interesting in this story is that completion represents not only the fact that matter in its various sharps and forms was created, but that the means for it to continue to thrive and multiply was a major part of it. Completion meant that all matter was equipped with the means to support itself in the acquisition of meeting all of the various needs that would arise. And this included humanity who was also given physical, mental, emotional, and spiritual needs to be filled in order to demonstrate a physical experience. The biblical account of everything being completed is said to be seven days. I assume this refers to cosmic days, which could be 100 million years per day or more, as we count literal days. But, using the story as metaphor, we can see that all of creation is interconnected and that nothing has been left out in terms of what's available to mankind and every living creature to meet every need. The New Thought movement's position on creation is that Spirit (God) became that which It created, since God is all there is there would be no other source to go to. In other words, God did not leave the confines of Its own Mind to create a physical universe, because that is the only place that exists where thoughts are transformed into expression. And if man is indeed created in the image of God, then man would create his reality in the same way, by thinking his thoughts into his reality. Look back over your life and think about something you gave serious thought to and how it materialized in your reality. This is why it is so important to learn how to control your thoughts and not let your thoughts control you. And by using the principles outlined in this book you will have learned how to control your thoughts to bring you the desired results you expect. Because you KNOW that It Is Already Done!

This session was the last of the principles Mr. Hill believed brought financial wealth to the people he followed. My expanded version was included in these principles, and I've also included an expansion to Mr. Hill's principles. So, from here on out, you will receive a bonus that was not included in the original material. Because this is not only about your financial success, but your overall well-being.

# PEACE – THE HIGHEST FORM OF MENTAL PLEASURE

HOW DOES ONE find peace in such a contentious world? First of all, you must recognize that peace is a state of mind and not a matter of doing something in order to obtain it. Simply put, there is nothing that exists outside of you that can initiate the process of bringing you into this state of being. However, there is something that you must do internally that will activate it. The acquisition of this state of being, as with all others, is an act of volition. It is an act of setting your will into motion. In other words, you must direct your will from one state of consciousness to another. When someone is said to have a strong will, it can be taken as a virtue if it is used to convert negative energy into positive energy. Negative energy is referred to here as energy that depletes the mind and body of good health. And conversely, positive energy is the revitalizing energy that produces a healthy mind and body. Your will is what determines your actions. In fact, determination is synonymous with the word will. In the previous session we dealt with setting your intentions or making your declarations of what it is you want out of life. Here, we are proclaiming that the proper use of your will, will in fact solidify your desires to your reality. Let's look at for a moment the difference between being strong-willed and being stubborn. A strong-willed person is one who seeks to bring about a result based on a conviction or strong belief that is held. In other words, a strong-willed person's conviction is not only at the conscious level, but also at the subconscious level. I guess you could say that the conscious mind has the backing of the subconscious mind when seeking to make what is believed to be an effective change. A stubborn person is one who generally seeks to keep things the same. Even in matters of change, the change for them must strongly resemble the current situation. In other words, stubborn people are generally concerned with their own selfish desires to have things their way, or not at all, despite whether they are acting on misinformation.

Take for example the reference to the civil rights movement. Those who were demonstrating for their civil rights were also demonstrating for human rights and they did so out of a conviction that portrayed segregation and discrimination as inhumane, immoral, and prejudicial. Their strong will is what prompted them to risk injury and even death to bring about the needed change they desired. The opposition on the other hand, were acting out of stubbornness. They did not want to make any changes because they were content with the current system of discrimination. It was what their forefathers had established, and they had been a part of for so long that they felt they would lose their superior social status if things were to change; so, they dug their heals in to try and preserve the status quo. But their stubbornness was not linked to a humanitarian cause, as was the demonstrators, and therefore the discriminators could not prevail. And although stubbornness is an act of the will, it is unsupportive of open-mindedness. Whereas, a strong-will is open to options that may bring about the desired results. It is the person who doesn't give up when one or several methods of accomplishing their mission fails. So, you could say that having a strong will can be an advantage when it comes to setting your intentions on bringing about changes in your life that you feel are desirable. But, a strong-will alone does not bring about the desires, it only supports your determination and persistence in taking the necessary steps toward your desires as you are guided by your sixth sense.

## Let There be Peace on Earth, and Let it Begin with Me

The reason I'm bringing in peace to this process is because that is the highest state of pleasure the mind can experience. And when the mind is in its most pleasurable state, it operates at its optimum level of envisioning and creating your highest version of yourselves. A strong-willed person is usually referred to as a stubborn person, who is so set in his ways that he refuses to listen to reason. However, you can be strong-willed without being stubborn. By this I mean, that in order for you to hold on to the ideas and concepts that will change your life for the better, you must have a strong constitution or strong-will. Because the temptation to go back to your old habits will rear-up when you can't see what's going on behind the scene, where Life (God) does Its work, and you want to think nothing is happening. This is a test of faith. Not that God tests your faith, you do. You have to test it in order to know that it's there. It's like test driving a car. You won't know what it's capable of doing until you get behind the wheel and take it for a spin. Your faith is the same way. The biblical definition of faith taken from Hebrews 11:1 is, "the assurance of things hoped for, a conviction of things not seen." You may have a slightly different definition, but it all boils down to knowing that something is happening that you desire when you can't see it happening. And it is my contention that this happens best, the exercising of faith, when your mind is at peace. The opposite of peace is chaos, worry, and confusion. So, how can you expect to hold on to your desires when your mind is filled with chaotic thoughts, worry, and confusion? That's why it is vitally important to be at peace with the world by not giving it your power by succumbing to worldly philosophies on how to live. One person summed up the worldly philosophies this way, "Get all that you can, can all that you get, then sit on the can!". Don't let that be the philosophy you ascribe to if you want to live a meaningful life.

# A Lot to Do About Nothing

We talked earlier about peace as being a key ingredient to healthy mind functioning. And we also spoke about how it is some-times tempting to want to go back to your former habits and ways of thinking when your faith gets shaky. Your peace can be disturbed by many different things such as, having a feeling that something just isn't right; or a perception that something is lacking; or something is not to your liking; or someone is out to get you, etc. When your peace is being gnawed away from these culprits, it's important to remember that there are two sides to every story. I'm speaking about the con-cept of relativity which we discussed previously and defined as the concept of polar opposites and your perceived relationship to them. Everything in your world is relative. Such as, the ups with its down, the hots with its cold, the lefts with its right, and so forth. So, in order to obtain peace, you must be willing to let go of the stories that are telling you that you can't have peace. Better still, the stories that you are telling yourself. These stories are usually from the past and you are bringing them forward. When you rehash those old stories that bring you grief, agitation, and confusion, you are slowly siphoning off your power of obtaining peace of mind.

Most of these stories are around something you did or didn't do, or something someone did to you, or something someone didn't do that you wanted them to do. Not only do you not have control over another person's actions, unless you're the parent of an underaged child; you cannot go back and change a single thing that has already been done. But, as we said before, you can change your perception of it, and not come from a victim's position. I recognize that many of the past stories that you tell yourself has some emotions association with it. These emotional part of the story serves as a reminder of what you should or shouldn't do if a similar situation presents itself. I get that. However, what I'm referring to when it comes to past stories is using them as an excuse not to move forward. I've told my kids stories from my past so that they could hopefully see the moral of the story and apply it to their own situations if necessary. But no present situation will be an exact replica of any past experience. Life is not stagnant, and therefore, you are not, or should not be the same person you were a short while ago. Not that your basic character need change, but when you are exposed to something new and you take something away from that exposure, then your perception shifts to make allowances for the new data.

## You Got To Give It Up

It's natural to experience every human emotion that you possess. But sometimes emotions are held on to a bit too long. Most often it's because you believe that your feelings may not have meant as much to you as you originally thought they did if you decide to let it go. It's like the grieving widow who grieves for her husband long after he's been gone. She probably had conflicting feeling when he passed away but felt guilty about that part of herself that actually felt relief when he died. So, she chose to believe that the grief she experienced would covered-up the relief part that she also felt. So, she kept right on grieving in order not to feel guilty for feeling relieved. This is an actual story that happened to a patient of mine. It was not until she was able to admit to herself that it was alright to have felt relief when her husband died, and therefore could let go of her grief without feeling guilty. By the way, her husband had suffered with Alzheimer's for years before he died, and she watched him slowly diminish in every capacity of normal functioning. How could she not feel a sense of relief when she saw the suffering of her husband come to an end. In essence, she was not so much grieving for him as she was for herself, and for her it turned into depression. So, letting go of the emotions associated with traumatic events, or even happy events can cause you to remain stuck in a pattern of thinking that does not propel you to move forward. Usually the more intense the emotion, the more the mind tends to want to hold on to those events that caused them. That's why there are literally thousands of people, especially veterans, who suffer from PTSD, post-traumatic stress disorder. The intensity of the emotions keeps the event alive. If you can imagine trying to go to sleep when your mind is racing at bedtime. You may be weary, but you can't shut your mind off because it has unresolved issues that won't allow it to shut down. This is what PTSD feels like when the mind has shocking vivid memories of some gruesome experiences that has yet to be resolved. It's like the mind asking "Why?" for answers that don't exist. People who can't sleep normally, usually end up taking sleeping pills. When the mind cannot disassociate from traumatic experiences it too needs a sedative. That sedative is a connection to the Source of All that Is. I'm not suggesting that you have to join some religious group in order to make this connection. I'm suggesting that there must be an acknowledgement of something greater than human strength or willpower to deal with traumas the mind can't handle. Some people blame the Source of All Things for the conditions that exist in the world. Their question is, "How could a loving God allow all the dreadful thing that go on in the world to happen?". If you happen to have read Rabbi Harold Kushner's ground-breaking book on this question, "When Bad Things Happen to Good People", you may have gotten some ideas as to why a Source with infinite knowledge permits things to happen the way they do. But, for our session I'll simply mention that mankind has been individually gifted with freewill. Because without freewill there can be no individuality. The freedom to make choices that supposedly reflects the character of the individual. However, sometimes that choice is used for good, and sometimes it isn't. So what we see happening in the world is the cumlative results of mans' choices. But no matter how it's used, it not only affects the individual, but it affects the whole human race, because we are all joined together by the same source, Life.

# ACTION – THE THING THAT GETS IT DONE

THE OLD SAYING that "actions speaks louder than words", is the operative statement that applies to everything you have learned from reading about the principles that leads to success. In other words, you must apply these principles to your everyday life in order to break the current mold that inhibits you from moving in the direction of getting your desires fulfilled. Together we have covered a lot of topics, all of which have the potential to change your life, which I'm surely hoping it will. And it may seem like it's a lot of work involved in making these changes. But it doesn't have to be arduous. It's like going back to school, but this time you're enrolling in the school of Life. It's the process of moving into the rhythm of life that supports you and your natural sense of well-being. It is what Sandra Ingerman writes about in her book, *Soul Retrieval*. She summaries the nature of her work as finding a cure for both personal and social ills through re-connection with the "field of energy that unites us all, and to bring back spiritual practices into our lives." And that is exactly what you are doing when you acknowledge a Higher Power at work in your life personally, and in the sustaining of the universe that supports your creativity. It was unfortunate that mankind moved away from meaningful spiritual practices when organized religion became big business and god became its biggest commodity. Most of what poses as spiritual practices is more like browbeating someone with a set of doctrines that are judgmentally based. And the practice of begging God to do something for you that God wouldn't ordinarily do unless you begged and groveled. And when God doesn't do what was asked, then the old safeguard is used that it must not have been according to God's will. Is this really what we expect our young people to buy into? In case you haven't noticed, there is a mass exodus of young people breaking away from the religious practices of their parents after they are old enough to excuse themselves. They are not to be blamed for wanting to experience a good life here on earth, rather than defer it until after they die. No loving parent would want that for their children, so why would God want to defer your being happy, prosperous, and content?

## The Immaculate Conception

For those of us who believe in a Higher Power, we must come to the understanding that our relationship with this entity we call God, Spirit, Divinity, Infinite Intelligence, or whatever name you choose to give It, is not based on superstitions, fears, or rewards and punishments. It's not even based on our behaviors, because behavior is merely a reflection of our thoughts. That's why the bible says, "Let this mind be in you that was also in Christ Jesus", meaning that it is your mind that controls your behavior, and the "Christ" consciousness is the consciousness that is focused on internal rather than external utterances. In order to change behaviors, you *must* change your way of thinking. To do otherwise would dishonor the purpose for which God created mankind, to enjoy and serve as guardians of the planet. However, one of the most important aspects of organized religion is that it is based on the acceptance of concepts which appears to be illogical, irrational, unreasonable, and even absurd to the human mind as valid. The reason why this is so important is because when you approach life from strictly a so-called logical, reasonable, rational point of view, you limit the depths of your imagination that creates separately from the data lodged in the part of your mind that relies on a process to try and figure things out. In other words, your imagination does not use the same so-called facts that the logical mind uses to reach its conclusions. Case in point, if you look at your bank statement and observe that a certain amount of money is there, and you would like more to be there. The logical mind would use the process of analyzing how that money got there in the first place, and that the means used previously must be replicated to get more there. In most cases, the logical mind may tell you that you *have to* go out and do some work to get more money. And this may result in you obtaining more money, assuming the work that you do is something someone is willing to pay you for. However, the imagination does not use analysis based on past experiences. It simply taps into your feelings and creates its scenarios from your desires. Imagine that! As the old saying goes, "If you can conceive it, you can achieve it". And it's more than just a nifty saying, it is the foundation of how the imagination works. It's not that the human mind does not enjoy entertaining the absurd and illogical. Hollywood certainly exploits the imagination with its portrayals of superhuman beings like Superman, Captain America, and other characters with extraordinary powers. But, when placed into the religious domain, portraying God with unlimited power seems to be illogical for some individuals. Given that this God supposedly has power over them, and not just over the bad guys like the super humans portray in the movies. Logic and reason does have its place, but not when it comes to the imagination.

## The Ayes Have It.

What's been said all along is that the *only* thing that separates you from your abundance is your thinking about what you have and what you are capable of having. The same holds true for the relationship you have with God. The only thing that separates you from God is *your* thought that you are separated. It's difficult for some people to imagine that God Almighty can and does live, and move, and has It's Being in them. They have dubbed themselves as being unworthy of God's blessings, so the thought that God resides within them is unthinkable. So, they go about the business of trying to become worthy by *doing* what they think God approves of. But what they fail to realize is that the thing God likes is for them to continue in their desire to become a highly evolved being that God can continue to create through. Everything God created is good, and it's up to us to use it for its intended purpose. And the way you do this is by being in harmony with your environment, after all you helped create it. It has been said that opportunity only knocks once. But I'm inclined to disagree. There is a biblical verse that speaks of opportunity knocking found in the book of Revelation 3:20, it says, "Behold, I stand at the door and knock: if any man hears my voice, and opens the door, I will come in to him, and will sup with him, and he with me." The "I" represents opportunity, and it continuously knocks at the door of your heart (feelings) and mind (thoughts) for you to open up to it and take full advantage of improving the things that brings good into your life and into the world. So, don't think that Life has passed you by no matter what age you are, or what condition you see yourself in, because your better days are before you. Including that big day when your spirit decides to leave the body for a higher pursuit. Life is cumulative, and it took every experience you've ever had to bring you to this place where you are now. And the rest of your experiences will add to your life exponentially now that you have grasped an inkling of Life's purpose and your relationship to It.

## Waiting on Godot

Finally, I could not leave our sessions without mentioning and quoting two of the most profound thinkers of modern times, one is Neville Goddard. His work is foundational in transformative thinking. Here's what he has to say about a universal law that most people probably do not even realize its existence. It is the law of reversibility. This law basically states that for every cause, there is an effect, and that the reverse is also true. Which means that every effect can create a cause.

He gives the examples of, "If heat can produce mechanical motion, so mechanical motion can produce heat. If electricity produces magnetism, magnetism too can develop electrical currents. If the voice can cause undulatory currents, so can such currents reproduce the voice, and so on.". Which is how we are able to hear voices on our radios. Goddard postulates that, "Cause and effect, energy and matter, action and reaction are the same and inter-convertible.". What this means is that if you knew how you would feel if you were in possession of the object of your desire, or how you would feel having accomplished what you would like to achieve, then inversely you would know what state you could realize were you to awaken in yourself such feeling. In other words, your feelings can play an important role in creating the state of mind necessary for you to accomplish and possess that which you desire. Once this feeling enters into your imagination it provides the Infinite Mind a mold to pour into it the substance that causes the manifestation of the image that created the feeling. It's an associative feeling that is linked specifically to an object or accomplishment that you desire. So, if you want a new place to live, imagine how you would feel upon unpacking your things and placing them into your new residence. I used to use this method when I was in the real estate business. When I knew I had found my clients the right home, I would ask them questions like, "on which wall will you be placing your sofa?", or "which room will you use for your bookcases?". When they started answering my hypothetical questions, I knew I had a sale. Because they saw themselves moving into that house and it *felt* like home to them. The more you grasp the concept of this law and use it as a means of manifesting your desires, the more you will accomplish in your life without putting forth a great deal of physical efforts.

## The Impersonal Life

The other person I must mention who probably has made the most profound impact on my life with his book, The Impersonal Life, is Joseph S. Benner. Here is what he has to say about unlocking the mysteries of attaining wisdom. "The Key is: To THINK is to CREATE. Or, as you THINK in your HEART, so is it with you. A Thinker is a Creator. A Thinker lives in a world of his own *conscious* creation. When you once know *how* "to think," you can create at will anything you wish, whether it be a new personality, a new environment, or a new world." What he's referring to is what I call Soul-Thinking. It is thinking from the perspective of living your life according to your Divine purpose and nature. It is centered around the unselfish desire to not only becoming the best person you can be, but also assisting others in their quest for the same. Each one, teach one. A quote by another one of the most profound thinkers of our time, Barbara Marx Hubbard, appropriately fits what I'm speaking about. She says, "Conscious Evolution signals the evolution of evolution itself from unconscious to conscious choice. It has occurred in our generation because humanity has gained the power to destroy our world, or to co-create cultures of immeasurable possibilities. It means that we are becoming conscious of our effect on evolution and must learn to guide our new powers toward a life-affirming future.". I take this statement to mean that we are on the cusp of extinction as a human race, or we are poised for distinction as a world of people who have figured out how to co-exist and support one another. Perhaps we will learn the latter from the effect from the coronavirus as we recognize our interdependence on each other. Hopefully, our sessions have assisted you in your comprehension of what it was that had been blocking you from your desires; and how to gain clarity in your declarations of what experiences you'd like to have in the expression of your personhood. You are the Captain of your Ship and the Master of your Fate, and you determine the direction and destination you travel as you set sail. The sea of life may get a little rocky sometimes, but keep in mind, your soul is anchored in the knowledge that you were made for this journey and nothing can impede your progress. If the only thing to fear is fear itself, then Know that perfect love casts out ALL fear. BE well and prosper!

**Namaste**

# EXPLORING THE CONCEPT OF GOD

WHEN ANSWERING THE following questions, you may want to write your answers on a piece of paper and read them back to yourself audibly so you can hear how they sound to you.

When I think of a higher power, do I believe it to be something that exists outside of myself, or within? Why do I feel this way?

When I was in my formative years, what do I recall being told about the existence of a Higher Power? What do I recall was my reaction?

What is my current concept of the existence of a Higher Power? If I believe there is a Higher Power, how do I think this affects my perception of myself? If I don't believe in a Higher Power how do I think this affects my self-perception?

If I do believe in a Higher Power, what do I think God's purpose was in creating me?

If I don't believe in a Higher Power, how do I think I came into this existence and for what purpose?

If I do believe in a Higher Power, what do I think I stand to gain or how am I benefitted by having this belief?

If I don't believe in a Higher Power, what do I think I would be giving up in order to hold such a belief? And what do I base this on?

If I do believe in a Higher Power, how do I reconcile the relationship between my freewill and God's sovereignty?

If I don't believe in a Higher Power how do I think the forces that energizes and sustains the universe influence my decisions about the care of the planet?

If I do believe in a Higher Power, what do I think is God's biggest concern regarding me and how I'm living my life? And what do I think God is doing about it, if anything?

If I don't believe in a Higher Power, what do I think about people who say they believe in God?

If I do believe in a Higher Power, when was the last time God communicated with me? What did God say or do that let me know it was actually God? How did it make me feel?

If I don't believe in a Higher Power, how did I establish my moral values? And what gives meaning to my life?

If I do believe in a Higher Power, do I truly believe that God loves and treats everyone the same? Or does God show favoritism toward those who acknowledge Her? If so, why? If not, why not?

If I don't believe in a Higher Power does that make it okay for me to discriminate against people who are different from me? If so, why? If not, why not?

If I do believe in a Higher Power, do I get offended when God is referred to as something other than the masculine, He or Him? Do I think God is offended by this also? If so, why? If not, why not?

If I don't believe in a Higher Power, do I get offended when God is referred to in a conversation with others? If so, why? If not, why not?

If I do believe in a Higher Power, there must be sufficient evidence of Gods' existence for me. What is this evidence that I have that sustains my believe in God?

If I don't believe in a Higher Power, what evidence would I need in order to change my belief?

If I do believe in God, do I feel it's my duty to tell others that they ought to do the same?

# EXPLORING YOUR RELATIONSHIP TO MONEY

What do I think about the statement, "The love of money is the root of all evil."?

What do I recall feeling when I first bought something using money?

How did my parent(s) (caregivers) treat money?

Did I receive an allowance growing up, or did I have to work outside the home to earn money? And what do I recall how I felt about that?

Do I consider myself wealthy or well-off or impoverished, or somewhere in-between? How did I come to this conclusion?

Am I envious of wealthy people?

Do I despise poor people, and think it's totally their own fault for their condition?

Do I believe that if I work hard enough I will have enough money?

Do I believe having a degree or certain credentials will obtain me more money than if I don't?

Do I feel I am paid what I am worth?

Do I enjoy what I do for pay?

Do I feel I deserve to live in abundance?

What does living comfortably mean to me? And do I use that as an excuse to settle for a lessor amount of money than I truly want?

Would I rather get a substantial raise on my job, or receive genuine praise from my superiors for the work that I perform?

What do I think about the statement, "Money doesn't grow on trees."?

What, if anything, is it about money that makes me feel uncomfortable?

What would I have done differently with my life if money weren't an issue?

What in my life would I change now, if money weren't an issue?

What scares me about not having enough money to live on once I'm through working?

What are some things that I was told about money that I later found out weren't true?

# AFFIRMATIVE STATEMENTS

This moment affords me infinite possibilities, for I live in the eternal now of being.

Everything I can possibly be is right this moment a part of my consciousness.

This moment I am prepared and equipped to accept my unlimited potential.

I am fully aware of my limitless capacity to be. My thinking is in the now; my vision is in the now; my anticipation is in the now.

My life is filled with wonderful people whose love and support is just what my experience calls for.

As I become more aware of my power of perception, I am also more aware of my will to perform that which I have been given.

I look to no one for my happiness, or for the good that comes into my life, but I recognize that everyone is a potential conduit through which Infinite Intelligence can bring good into my life.

As I am one with Infinite Intelligence, my consciousness has in it all ideas, concepts, and knowledge. I know what I need to know at the very moment I need to know it. This knowing annihilates all ignorance from my subconscious mind.

I Am intelligence, power, and love in perfect balance.

Within my consciousness is the clarity I need to produce the desires of my heart.

This moment and every moment moves smoothly for me because I am confident and efficient as I allow the Divine Orchestrator to motivate and activate my consciousness.

My actions are the natural outgrowth of my awareness. I am successful in all of my undertakings because I am competent in addressing every area of my life.

I am constantly and continually receptive to new ways and methods for my greatest good to unfold.

I am creative in my approach to life and the many ways that I show up, and I know that my creativity comes from within.

I am mentally and emotionally dedicated to my own good and to the good of others. I live in a friendly universe filled with an abundance of everything I could possibly want or need, and it responds effortlessly to my healthy desires.

Without conceit, I can honestly say that I am spiritually perfect. I have a healthy consciousness and I enjoy it. I have no fears and no regrets, I am vitally alive right now. And I am totally self-confident.

# COMMONLY USED EXCUSES FOR NOT SUCCEEDING

TO THOSE WHO practice the art of failing, the most meaningful word in their vocabulary is, IF. And here are some of the ways they use it.

IF I didn't have the responsibility of taking care of a wife and family . . .

IF I had enough influence with the right people . . .

IF I had money . . .

IF I had a better education . . .

IF I could get a good job . . .

IF my health were better . . .

IF I only had time . . .

IF times were better . . .

IF my parents would have given me . . .

## IS THERE SOMETHING YOU WANT?

IF other people understood me better . . .

IF conditions around me were only different . . .

IF I were of a different nationality . . .

IF I could live my life over again . . .

IF I did not fear what "they" would say about me . . .

IF I had been given a chance . . .

IF I now had a chance . . .
IF other people weren't out to get me . . .

IF there weren't so many obstacles in my way . . .

IF I were only younger . . .

IF I hadn't wasted so many good years . . .

IF I could only do what I want . . .

IF I had been born wealthy . . .

IF I could meet the "right" people . . .

IF I had the talent that some people have . . .

IF I only knew how to assert myself . . .

IF I would have taken advantage of past opportunities . . .

IF people didn't annoy me so much . . .

## COMMONLY USED EXCUSES FOR NOT SUCCEEDING

IF I could save some money . . .

IF I were appreciated by those who are around me . . .

IF I only had somebody to help me . . .

IF my family were more understanding . . .

IF I lived in a more progressive place . . .

IF the "powers that be" didn't inhibit my choices . . .

IF my personality were different . . .

IF I weren't so fat . . .

IF people only knew what I am capable of . . .

IF I could catch a break . . .

IF I could only get out of debt . . .

IF I hadn't failed previously . . .

IF I only knew how to . . .

IF I didn't have so many things to worry about . . .

IF I were in a relationship with the right person . . .

IF other people weren't so stupid . . .

IF I had more self-confidence . . .

# IS THERE SOMETHING YOU WANT?

IF I didn't have so much bad luck . . .

IF I weren't a Gemini, or Taurus, or Aquarius, etc. . . . .

IF I didn't have to work so hard . . .

IF I hadn't lost that money . . .

IF I only had a business of my own . . .

IF my business didn't require me to work 12-hour days . . .

IF I could just find the motivation to get started . . .

IF I truly believed that the principles given in this book could really change my life . . .

IF*** and this is the biggest IF of them all ... *if* I had the courage to see myself as I really am, and I would find out what is wrong with me and correct it. Then I might have a chance to profit from my mistakes and learn something from the experiences of others. Because I know that there is something wrong with me, or I would now be where I would have been if I had spent more time analyzing my weaknesses and correcting them, and less time building alibis to try to cover them up.

All of these excuses, and there are many more than these, are used to cling to that which supposedly justifies one's actions, or lack thereof. And people hold on to their excuses of choice because they created them in their own imagination. And remember we said that the subconscious mind does not make a distinction between fact and fiction, so it acts upon that which you insist is true. And to those who use excuses for their failure to achieve what they desire most these excuses appear real. Also keep in mind what we said about being creatures with habits. Making excuses is habitual and it uses the same energy that is used to make affirmations. Both come from a decision you've made based on a belief that you hold about yourself.

So, one of the biggest questions you'll ever face is, "What are you willing to give up in order to gain something greater?" Because unless you are willing to cross the bridge from your current condition over into your new one, and burn that bridge behind you, you will remain where you are. Because you will never become totally committed to your new condition as long as you continue to see your old condition as an option to run back to if the new one fails.

You are already a success, so think it, feel it, and proclaim it as you demonstrate the awesome person that you are!

Lightning Source UK Ltd.
Milton Keynes UK
UKHW021450070720
366156UK00014B/1519